TEACHING YEAR TWO

Edited by Lucy Hall

Published by Scholastic Ltd.
Villiers House
Clarendon Avenue
Leamington Spa
Warwickshire CV32 5PR

Text © 1998 Paul Noble; George Hunt; Peter Clarke; Terry Jennings;
Margaret Mackintosh; Dorothy Tipton; Gillian Robinson; Pauline Boorman; Richard Ager;
Lynn Newton; Douglas Newton; Geoffrey Teece
© 1998 Scholastic Ltd.

90   4567

Authors

Paul Noble, George Hunt, Peter Clarke, Terry Jennings, Margaret Mackintosh,
Dorothy Tipton, Gillian Robinson, Pauline Boorman, Richard Ager, Lynn Newton,
Doug Newton, Geoffrey Teece

Series Editor
Lucy Hall

Editor
Kate Pearce

Series Designer
Lynne Joesbury

Designer
Rachel Warner

Illustrations
Ray and Corinne Burrows

Cover photograph
Fiona Pragoff

Designed using Adobe Pagemaker

British Library Cataloguing-in-Publication Data
A catalogue record for this book is available from the British Library

ISBN 0 590 53820 9

The publishers acknowledge and thank the following for the use of copyright material:
National Curriculum 2000 © The Queen's Printer and Controller of HMSO. Reproduced under the terms of HMSO Guidance Note 8. © Qualifications and Curriculum Authority. Reproduced under the terms of Guidance Note 8. National Literacy and Numeracy Documents © Crown Copyright. Reproduced under the terms of HMSO Guidance Note 8. Early Learning Goals © Qualifications and Curriculum Authority.

Scholastic Ltd. thank Roland Smith for the use of the poster on page 42.

Contents

Preface

Primary school teachers don't say, as secondary teachers would, 'I teach history'. They say 'I teach year 4s' or 'I teach a reception class'. Why, then, have all the books for primary teachers been wholly subject-orientated? Primary teachers have had to buy about 13 different books and read through them all to extract the relevant bits.

It was about 20 years ago that the thought occurred to me that it would make teachers' lives much easier if all the information about teaching their year group was provided in *one* book. Since then I have been waiting for someone to do it. But no-one did. So, finally, fourteen different authors, Scholastic and I have put together the seven *Primary Teacher Yearbooks.*

I should like to thank all the authors. They faced a difficult task in tailoring their writing to a common format and structuring their guidance, about what to teach and what to expect from children, so that it correlated with the seven different stages of the primary school. They have all been extremely patient.

Particular thanks are due to Paul Noble, who not only wrote 13 chapters in the series, but was also deeply involved in the development of the project from the very beginning. His practical, knowledgeable advice and cheerful imperturbability kept the whole project stuck together.

We all hope that you will find your Yearbook useful and that it meets your needs – whichever class you teach.

Lucy Hall, Series Editor

Your Class

Year 2 is a delightful age-group to teach and you should gain a great deal of satisfaction from your class in spite of the fact that it is also the year which is constrained by SAT requirements. Open your classroom door in the morning and the children will enter, pleased to see you and to be there. You should be able to encourage their growing self-confidence, willingness to please and ever-developing academic skills. And if the SATs do disconcert you, be comforted, for by and large the children will not turn a hair.

Organising your classroom

Simple is the key word when making preparations for this class. For example, do not make piles of things. With Year 2s, rulers must be next to pencils which must be next to something else – not stacked one on top of the other. If you heap jigsaws in piles and expect children to be able to select and use them properly you will be disappointed.

When organising a Year 2 class it is important to give children direct choices – either this or that. Children will still need to be instructed in the layout of the classroom, but the availability of opportunities for learning, as well as access to materials, will be no different from any other Key Stage 1 class. Nevertheless, in preparing the classroom you must take account of the children's ability to understand instructions only if they are kept simple. 'Bags go here, lunch boxes go there'. Simple instructions, simple choices.

Flat level areas are at a premium when it comes to displaying equipment and work because almost everything must be at child-eye level. If you have to display a number line, for example, above this level its use and impact will decline dramatically. Displays above head height will make good wallpaper but will be of little use otherwise. The same applies to notices and pictures. If your school has a Picasso on loan from the Tate, it must be displayed low down where it can be touched and seen or it may never be properly appreciated.

Games and equipment for gross motor activities and play virtually disappear from the Year 2 class although the need for tactile experiences – claywork, weighing, painting, and so on – is undiminished, as is the need for creative play. What does change is the need for undirected experimentation, now it is vital that an element of intellectual challenge is included. More space will be required for wordbanks and dictionaries, tape recorders and computers (at least two, it is to be hoped), science and experimentation corners, maths tables and, of course, books.

Children must have their own space and their own storage drawer, desk or shelf, and there should be enough furniture to enable all the class to be seated simultaneously at desks or tables. Carpet space is desirable but it must be accepted that the space available for 'carpet time' is likely to be more restricted than for a reception class. A great deal must be squeezed into the classroom and the floor space required is as great as at any time in the child's schooling especially if you follow the 'no stacking' rule.

Unless you are very familiar with the room and its contents, a preparatory stock check is

recommended. List equipment according to subjects, then further sub-divide the lists into useful categories such as furniture; games; expendables; tools, and so on. This will prepare you for the rest of the year and you will avoid the nasty surprise of finding out, after you have unpacked the equipment, that you have not got the space for it!

The argument for having tables grouped in blocks to provide large working spaces and opportunities for talk are at their strongest in Key Stage 1, and it is unusual to find other arrangements such as rows. However, whatever decision you make about this, think first about your pupils and what you want the seating arrangement to do for them as well as for you. Make sure you arrange furniture to facilitate your literacy and numeracy hour work. Can all the children see the board without shifting tables and chairs? Can you easily arrange the tables for group activities?

The first day

On the first day (and subsequently every day if you wish) collect the children together on the carpet and begin from there. 'Name games' are a good way to start as this gives you a chance to mark the register and at the same time begin to identify each child by name (you may, of course, already be familiar with the children). You might, for example, give out pre-prepared labels for each child to wear (and one for yourself) or get the children to make them as the first exercise of the day.

Another choice is to play a memory game. One child says 'I am David Smart (or whatever his or her name is) and I have a cut on my knee.' The next child makes his or her statement but also repeats the previous one. 'I am Mamiko Mori and I wear glasses. He is David Smart and he has a cut on his knee.' And so on.

You might also try a Guess-the-Child game. 'I see someone with a ponytail, a shiny watch and their arms folded. Who is it?' The children can join in by setting the questions.

Establishing ground rules

By Year 2, parents should understand the rules of the school and not be monopolising your time when they bring their child to school in the morning. Generally, it is better if children are greeted at the door and separated from parents there, but parents and children should, by Year 2, be doing this of their own volition. If there are exceptions (a particularly nervous or insecure child) then work out a programme to gradually wean the child, and parent, to independence. Children of this age should not need mum to hang up their coat or carry their lunch box for them.

Establishing the ground rules for operating your class is not a task to be treated lightly although, as most of the children will have been at the school for two years, you will have

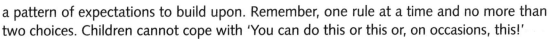

a pattern of expectations to build upon. Remember, one rule at a time and no more than two choices. Children cannot cope with 'You can do this or this or, on occasions, this!'

There are always unanswered questions when a child encounters a new teacher and a new class. The child may be looking forward excitedly to meeting you or may be apprehensive. During the first few days and weeks you must gain the children's confidence and try gradually to reassure them about issues that they find worrying. The list of concerns will be shorter than it was in Year 1 and Reception – they will probably know by now where the toilets are and the rules about using them – but some issues will still remain and you may not do things quite in the way their previous teacher did even where you have agreed a common strategy. These little things are important when you are six or seven.

Consider the following:

- What is the procedure for going to the toilet during lessons?
- Where can they play at playtime?
- Which entrances are they allowed to use?
- Which areas are 'out-of-bounds'?
- What do they do with their lunch boxes?
- Where do they sit?
- Which is their drawer?
- Where do they put their PE kit?
- Have they got their names on their sweatshirts and other clothing?
- How do they get teacher's attention?
- Are there any rules for moving around the classroom?
- Who can touch the computers and when?
- Where are the tissues for the runny noses? May they help themselves?
- What about fire drill and emergency exits?
- Clearing-up? Who does what and when?
- What should they keep in their drawers?
- Can they bring pencils to school?
- What are the rules about using rubbers and scissors?
- Teacher's desk – what rules apply?

It is by no means straightforward to establish all the rules you want children to observe. Broad 'catch-all' principles and rules are undoubtedly best for this age-group even though they may seem somewhat vague to adults. Making lots of specific rules to cover many eventualities only confuses a seven-year-old and, of course, you can't cover everything. However, you can always measure a specific behaviour against a global rule. *You kicked Sean. Now was that a kind thing to do?* Gradually, children can be led to measuring behaviour for themselves, provided the general principles are clearly established in the first place. Establish them by explaining, by demonstration, by enforcement and by example.

What can I expect of Year 2 children?

The type of school in which you are teaching Year 2s makes a difference. In infant schools they are top dogs, trusted and feted responsibility-takers; in all-through primary schools the long shadow cast by their junior co-habitants does sometimes inhibit their ambition and lower the status accorded them by teachers – although the children are, of course, exactly the same creatures. Awareness of this will ensure that your expectations are appropriate.

In infant-only schools Year 2s tend to become more independent because more is expected of them and they start to take responsibility for younger children if they see them distressed or in trouble. This is a reaching out for maturity (not to be confused with the real thing). 'Can I collect the books, Miss?' The Year 2 child is eager to be grown up, but this eagerness to help can quickly turn into clamour because the Year 2 lacks self-restraint and will still nag like a young infant.

Expect your Year 2 child to be a bit of a prig at times. 'Miss said not to do that! I'm telling.' Year 2s live in a world in which there is a general acceptance of rules imposed from the outside. 'Teacher said' may be sufficient for a six- to seven-year-old but they are still able to compare sets of rules and to accept reasons for them. In behaviour, as in matters academic, you are moving the Year 2 child towards independence.

As independence grows, you will be able to operate systems in the classroom that require independent responsible action and the children will be able to carry this responsibility outside the classroom as well. They will collect the bell, return the registers to the office, and so on. They will actively seek these jobs and you must be careful only to give them tasks that are safe and within their capabilities (no returning teacups to the staffroom!).

Relationships

Year 2 children are just beginning to be aware of gender although the awareness is, perhaps, subconscious. Big groupings of children will happily be mixed although, if they are playing or working in small groups, these will tend to be single sex, mainly because life presents them with fewer problems that way. They will identify with groups of various sorts and have begun to think beyond themselves as individuals.

Awareness of sex also makes itself manifest although the awareness is usually giggly and non-comprehending. A little girl will come up to you at playtime clutching the hand of a little boy from her class. 'Miss, Hanif's my boyfriend.' Then with a few cheerful and unembarrassed giggles they will skip off to play. They are aware of something in this boy-girl thing but they are uncertain as to what it is. 'Ugh! Jenny kissed me, Miss!' This attitude will even appear in their stories irrationally and unannounced '...and then the fairy got married.' Some children will have learnt the animal facts of life through their pets or whatever but will make no natural connection with themselves. The seven-year-old has simply learnt the healthy outlet known as the giggle.

Children with special needs

Year 2 is often the first year in which sustained effort and resources are applied to the problem of special needs children. Partly this happens for practical reasons (it is about targeting scarce resources) and partly it is because judgements have begun to firm up about those children within the normal range (stage 1 to stage 4 of the Code of Practice) of school provision. As the new class teacher do not be too hasty in making judgements about SEN designation in the first few weeks.

Of course there will be children in your classroom with a range of differing special needs, some will be educational but others will be physical, emotional, social or behavioural. Assume that you can cater for them all – any other counsel is a counsel of despair. Nevertheless, there will broadly be two groups of pupils and problems: those whom you can help and those for whom the real solution lies outside the school.

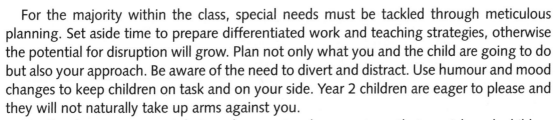

For the majority within the class, special needs must be tackled through meticulous planning. Set aside time to prepare differentiated work and teaching strategies, otherwise the potential for disruption will grow. Plan not only what you and the child are going to do but also your approach. Be aware of the need to divert and distract. Use humour and mood changes to keep children on task and on your side. Year 2 children are eager to please and they will not naturally take up arms against you.

Use the classroom support that you have, or involve parents, so that special needs children have the language support and the one-to-one attention that they require. Very able children, as well as less able children, need to be purposefully employed. It is a good idea when setting up your classroom displays to include activities (on the 'tinkering table' or maths and writing areas) that can be done when the set activity has been completed. Generally you cannot afford to use the computer as a quality occupier in this way but if you have a particular problem child you may not be able to afford not to!

For those children for whom you lack resources, or for whom the solution lies outside the classroom or your ability to handle, you must seek help (from the parents, the headteacher, the SENCO) while using your skills as a teacher to contain or divert the child in the classroom. At this level, outside agencies will almost certainly be involved, but a word of warning. While it is sensible to work on the assumption that learning or behavioural problems can be solved within the classroom through careful planning and preparation, this assumption is not a universal truth. Occasionally problems do occur which you can't solve – no matter how good a teacher you are. You will best help yourself and the child by recognising this fact and identifying, if you can, the possible causes of intractable problems. Be alert for medical problems, emotional disturbance, child abuse, and so on. Always share your problems with someone and do not take the failure personally.

Mobile children

There may be special groups within your class (travellers, service children, foreigners) but essentially their needs are the same as any other child in the class. Do not treat them as in any way odd or respond to stereotypical images. Dealing with a non-English speaking child of a Japanese businessman in Britain for six months does pose practical problems somewhat different from those posed by the child of an RAF sergeant who has moved three times in a year, but both children need reassurance, attention and appropriate work, as well as to feel happy and secure.

ESL children

Non-English speaking children pose a particular problem but experience of dealing with them is considerable and your LEA will be a good source of advice and support. Ultimately, bilingual children can be an asset to the school so do not worry when you first meet them. Schools dealing with large numbers of non-English speaking children usually have special provision and expertise that enables them to cope (language assistants, for example) Usually children who started school in your reception class as non-English speakers will, by Year 2, have already acquired enough functional English to operate quite happily with their English peers.

However exceptional a child's needs may seem to you, there will be established patterns of good practice which you can follow. Seek advice. Your headteacher can contact outside agencies if necessary.

Health and disability problems

Although physical disability poses problems in schools it has social and educational spin-offs that are positive. Children and teachers gain insights into the lives of others and to 'walk a mile in the moccasins of another tribe' is one of the most valuable and life-enhancing lessons one can learn. As with bilingualism there is plenty of advice and support available via your LEA. Make sure you consult them. Involve your Health and Safety governor in checking that the physical environment poses no especial hazard or unacceptable restriction to the disabled child. Occasionally, expensive adaptation may be required (a lift perhaps) but the problem will have to be dealt with. Where physical disability is involved, the parents are likely to have made themselves experts in their child's needs, so be sure to liaise with them.

Asthma is now such a common complaint that the management of inhalers and other medicines is becoming a problem in schools and new requirements will soon be in operation. Children on medication will require their own medical educational plan on which the medication and its administration is described and this will need to be approved by parents. However your school chooses to manage these new legal requirements, commonsense dictates that medicines should never be stored casually in the classroom. Ideally several (if not all) members of staff will have received instruction in dealing with asthma so that the storage and regular use of inhalers can be properly organised. Make sure you are adequately informed.

Problems at home

Emotionally children are laying the bedrock of their later lives at this age, and insecurity and unhappiness experienced at seven can stay with them and influence the kind of adults that they will become. Sometimes some quite traumatic event may be dealt with in a matter-of-fact way, but do not underestimate the inner hurt. 'My granny died yesterday, Miss.' Death is dealt with as a piece of information, spoken about but not lingered over. Grief is another matter. Emotional tension at home due to a death, a birth or a festering marital problem will upset any young child and at seven they are particularly vulnerable.

T. S. Eliot spoke of three pivotal experiences in life, 'birth, copulation and death' and directly or indirectly these will affect young children. At seven their greatest reaction is perhaps to their parents' reactions to these things; parental grief is often harder to bear than the matter being grieved over.

Deal with these matters by allowing children the opportunity to talk when they want to. Be honest and open. It helps children if we share our puzzlement with them about life's confusions and to talk about the few clues that we have. It rarely helps to be judgemental but the child has a right to know where we stand. Extreme behaviour (violence in the home, for example) may be condemned but in a way that focuses on the behaviour not the person. This helps to limit the confusion in the child's mind.

Watch out for signs of emotional stress. A child who becomes withdrawn or violent, whose work dramatically declines in quality or who starts to steal is usually drawing attention to him or herself in a way that should alert you. These are the kind of signs that may be exhibited when a mother starts to go out to work or when a father loses his job. Any number of events can trigger this behaviour but particularly any upsets involving the child's parents. At seven children still prefer that the last person they see when they go into school and the first person they see when they come out is mum or dad.

Home-school issues

Parents will have stressed that the child should never go with strangers. Although young children are naturally vulnerable for all sorts of obvious reasons, it is nevertheless true that they will not naturally go with another person. Children will even resent a well-liked and known childminder and 'play up' if they were expecting mum to collect them. Both you and the parents must make sure that children understand the rules about never going with strangers.

Working with parents or carers is the best way to cope with many of the problems that you may encounter with a particular child but it is important to involve them when things go right as well as when things go wrong. Good communication is essential, although some parents will wish to be involved in the classroom. This can be a great help but remember you are in charge and are responsible for the class. Do not impose a disruptive parent on other people's children!

Standard Assessment Tasks

Few pretend any more that SATs do not make a difference and Year 2 is a year where this difference is most keenly felt. They will also affect your relationship with parents who will ask about SATs and express concerns about them.

It is best to get them involved from the beginning. Some schools have special parents' evenings early in the year to do just this. Many parents will ask what they should be doing at home and the answer is: in general, support and encourage – as they would at any stage in the child's career – and, specifically, help their child with maths and literacy when the opportunity arises. This will occur when the child takes his reading book home; when he is asked to memorise his number bonds; or practise some spellings. The need for parental support and practice at home is very important, as is the need to avoid overloading and pressurising the child so that he learns to hate reading, school, the National Curriculum, and any form of learning.

Parental help with homework will be more effective if you explain precisely what is expected of them. Have a session giving some basic instruction in how to listen to a child read. Explain to them the 'look, cover, write, check' strategy for the teaching of spelling. Encourage them to share a book with their child for pleasure every night.

Regular liaison with parents will avoid those sudden explosive problems that can be such a psychological strain and it is equally important, for similar reasons, that long-term concerns are shared with them early on. If a child is likely to get 'working towards level 1' then this is best explained to parents as soon as possible. Skating round issues like this only makes it worse in the end.

Transferring to the juniors

At one time parental concern about seven-year-olds focused on their imminent transfer to the juniors. This has generally been replaced by concern about SATs. However, where there is a physical transfer involved to another school, child and parents will need reassurance. There are few junior schools which do not invite infant parents to meetings at the school before the term commences and most prepare the ground pretty well.

If the transfer is within the same school, there are likely to be very few concerns. Children, generally, look forward to the change. Big school means big status. Junior school is sometimes

used as an incentive by parents and teachers but, obviously, it should *never* be used as a threat – even indirectly (*Do you think that juniors would only write three lines, Craig?*). It is worth pointing out – in the summer, not before – where junior work might differ (joined writing, perhaps) or expectations vary (such as school uniform) as this helps to demystify the move.

Behaviour and personal development issues

Year 2s are beginning to develop a sense of moral outrage. When something happens that conflicts with the simple rules that they have grown to accept they will openly object - which is why one of the most overheard phrases in a Year 2 class is usually 'I'm telling!' Seven-year-olds react directly to events and feelings as they occur. Systematic bullying, which by common understanding usually involves forethought and persistent malice, is not something that Year 2s will generally do. Of course the actions associated with bullying do happen. Year 2 children will hit each other, will refuse to play with someone or call each other names, but rarely with any malice or persistence and will quickly switch from anti behaviour to pro. Keep to the basic rule of comparing the child's behaviour with the general rule (*Was that a kind thing to do?*) and never ignore any bad behaviour, particularly violent behaviour, whatever name you choose to give it. Extremely violent behaviour is always a sign of emotional disturbance and unlike bullying will not be directed solely at one individual.

The seven-year-old is easily reduced to tears still. Confronted with a simple searching question (*James, I think you have something to tell me*) the child will usually reveal what has happened. Be patient and insistent and the child will confront himself with his own wrong-doing. When dealing with bad behaviour the rule 'simple is best' again applies. Year 2 children can understand and will respond to a simple rule such as 'It takes two to do something wrong.' (Even if not strictly true it is amazing how often invoking this rule will sort a problem out. *So, Lily hit you? But what did **you** do, David?*)

Rewards

You will need a reward system, and it must be one that is generous. Children with low self-esteem or who perform at a poor academic level need to be able to earn approval often. Children who are the subject of a behaviour-management programme must earn lots of 'stars' easily and lead on to a carefully calculated reward (being given time to play a favourite game or whatever). The award needs to have some value to the child. (One infant teacher allowed 'good' children to place their hands under a running tap! It was regarded as a big treat - and it worked!)

Difference

Year 2s are curious about difference. They will notice Mr Janner's new tie, Natalie's broken arm, Gary's glasses and Kalim's brown skin, but their curiosity will be expressed in exactly the same way: teacher's new tie is no more or less interesting than Kalim's skin colour. A few questions and away they will skip. Malice, if it occurs, will usually have been learned. Confront the undesirable behaviour as you would any other – never let it pass without comment. But building up a caring ethos and respect for all human beings is ultimately the positive way to prevent anti-social behaviour from occurring. Racism, sexism, and bullying are matters best dealt with through prevention rather than cure.

Curriculum and Classroom Planning

Making plans

Curriculum planning is not exclusively a way of making sure that you do not forget anything, it is also a way of making sure that you do not try to cover too much or do too many things simultaneously. Good teachers, therefore, do it intelligently. The best advice is to be brief, be selective and, above all, be realistic. Because of the demands of OFSTED, most teachers equate curriculum planning with planning for delivering content which, following what is now the most widely accepted model, comes down to *long-term*, *medium term* and *short term* plans. Whichever class you are teaching, this planning framework will be the same.

Long term plans

Long term plans are the broad outline of work across the whole year. This can be done well in advance (the preceding summer term, usually) and should be easy and relatively enjoyable. Easy because it should be the result of directly transferring material from the school's schemes of work, and enjoyable because you will be able to make some choices about the type of projects, visits and programmes that you would like to be engaged in this coming year. With Year 2s you must leave time in your long term plans for SATs and for any practice material you intend to do leading up to the testing period. Do long term planning early (your school may well use a pro-forma sheet) and do not waste time on detail. Write too little rather than too much.

Medium term plans

Medium term plans require more detail. These plans deal with the term's work or, more commonly, with the half-term's work. You are in charge of your class and you must judge whether your children are ready to do one hour of maths, two hours of maths – or none at all. Having said that, there are now enormous pressures on you to package your teaching in specific ways. The Literacy and Numeracy Hours are obvious examples. Although much of this pressure comes in the form of 'guidance' with OFSTED breathing down your neck, it is, unfortunately, guidance that you ignore at your peril.

Your school will have examined the suggestions from QCA and taken account of them in the structuring of its schemes of work so you will have some kind of framework to work with, but it is still for you to decide when to undertake one activity rather than another.

(During a maths lesson, my Year 2s were surprised by a helicopter making an emergency landing in the playground directly outside the classroom window. No matter how hard I tried to focus the children's attention on sums, the maths lesson was doomed – but the lesson that took its place took off as swiftly as the helicopter.)

As this is a practical guide to running a class, we will put aside theoretical plans which apportion every second of the day to the curriculum. Research has shown that teachers grossly underestimate the amount of time spent on non-teaching activities: transfers from room to room; registration; clearing up; toileting; sorting out behaviour problems; looking for lost property; listening to children; talking to them; interruptions by the headteacher; the school nurse; school assemblies; and so on. You can, no doubt, think of many others. Many of these activities may have educational value but they are not subjects in the National Curriculum. In practice, you will probably have no more than three hours of curriculum time available each day. The following model is intended to help you face the real world and draw up plans balanced as your school (or QCA) think fit.

A balanced teaching plan

Setting aside all non-curriculum activities leaves around 16 hours available per week.

English	Maths	Science	Physical PE/dance/games	Creative Art/DT/music	Humanities RE/History/Geography
6	4	2	1.5	2	0.5

(Note: At Key Stage 1 the Numeracy 'Hour' suggested is, in fact, 45 minutes.)

This would clearly be an unsatisfactory plan if the same pattern were followed each week, so there has to be a variation of emphasis within topic work (science/humanities). Think of the balance over the long term rather than the short term. You must keep physical activities going on a regular basis or you are wasting your time. Young children also need the release from the academic that the creative subjects provide. ICT and some English teaching will take place through other subjects.

Over a few weeks, the balance might look like this:

English	Maths	Science	Physical	Creative Art/DT/music	Humanities RE/History/Geography
6	4	2	1.5	2	0.5
6	4	2	1.5	2	0.5
6	4	0	1.5	2.5	3
6	4	0	1.5	2.5	3
6	4	1	1.5	2	2.5
6	4	1	1.5	2	2.5

Over six weeks the curriculum is divided: 37.5% English; 25% Maths, 6.23% Science, 9.4% Physical; 13.5% Creative and 12.5% Humanities. There is no magic in these figures but they are rooted in reality – change the balance to suit yourself.

Short term plans

Short term plans cover the day-to-day management of your teaching in the classroom. *What am I going to do today? What broadcast am I watching? What work is to be done by the special needs children and when? What is the classroom support assistant going to do? Are there any visitors, festivals or other disruptions to the routine such as visits by the school photographer or the nurse?* You will have your own agenda of things to do. You may have a behaviour programme to undertake with a disruptive pupil; a school assembly to practise; a student to tutor; work to do as part of your subject co-ordinator's role; meetings with parents and a health education plan to produce. Short term plans are notepad-and-pencil plans and fit alongside your timetable which sets the time framework for everything that you do. (Don't forget to note down your playground duty week and when you have to wash up in the staffroom!) Some school managements regard these short term plans as private documents, other heads will wish to see copies of them. OFSTED inspectors like to know that this kind of daily planning goes on but do not always demand to see evidence.

Getting organised

Planning is not only about sorting out what you are going to teach: you will need to think about the materials and resources that you are going to need and, to some extent, how you are going to use them.

Resources

The range of resources available to you, provided your school can afford them, is quite overwhelming. Libraries and museums, commercial suppliers, specialist bodies, subject associations, advisory groups, LEA support services and even the DfEE are sources of advice, sometimes physical help and, most often, materials. Where do you start? You will have

started by making your curriculum plans and deciding on the topics and subjects that you wish to cover. You also know when these will be being taught. Next you should make a decision about what materials can be provided in-house. Your subject co-ordinators will help and have probably already produced resource lists as part of the school's schemes of work. Follow these normal procedures and then check through the school's drawers and cupboards – schools nearly always have more equipment than the staff are aware of (weaving looms discarded when a teacher left three years ago; a binocular microscope lost in a stock cupboard – these are real examples). Next, decide what you will expect the children to provide. Your Victorian project may end up being resourced almost entirely from objects brought in by the children. Similarly, topics on colour or materials can be almost fully resourced from home. When you have done this you can look towards museums, galleries, and so on to fill gaps in your resources. With Year 2s, you will require a rich supply of reading materials and you may depend heavily on the library service for this but, as the National Curriculum takes you over similar ground every year, you should find that the school's need for outside resources reduces as it acquires its own materials. Be aware that you can have too many resources. Year 2s can get a great deal out of very little and, if you overwhelm them with objects, they will be confused in the same way that you will be if you have too much advice and materials on how to teach 'Water'. Be selective and aim for quality rather than quantity.

Audio-visual aids

The advice regarding audio-visual aids in the classroom is very similar. Only have as much on display as you can cope with. You may, in any case, be limited by the number of sockets available, especially if your classroom is an old one. Two computers is about the standard for a Year 2 class, although the world of ICT changes quickly. Keep the software you are going to use to hand and do not become immersed in the rest. The effective use of a few programmes is better than the confusion of excess. Make sure that you have some method of recording computer and other audio-visual use – perhaps a tick chart by the side of the relevant machine. You must decide for yourself which additional equipment you will employ, but Year 2 children can make good use of tape recorders coupled with a distribution box and headphones and more specialist equipment such as the Language Master.

Competence certificates

Decide if your are going to allow the children to switch on the machines. The answer may well be 'No', but one strategy is to train children to different levels of competence and issue them with certificates celebrating their skill. At Year 2 this may not go far beyond: 1) Can push in a wall plug correctly. 2) Can switch on the computer. 3) Can switch off the computer (more difficult!). Further up the school children may already be becoming competent with the Internet. It may be useful to agree a whole-school policy on competence certificates.

Visits and visitors

Visits and visitors are essential. Ideally at least one out-of-school visit per term. Clearly, expensive visits involving travel over long distances cannot be as frequent as this, but aim for as many visits as is feasible. Remember, however, that the value of the outing diminishes with the distance travelled. Visits must be well-planned; an advance visit beforehand is virtually essential; and every visit must be tightly focused. Make sure that you do not

trundle your seven-year-olds around the entire British Museum, or travel sixty miles to an arboretum when there is a perfectly good park ten minutes from the school.

Visiting is a two-way exchange

When you plan for a visitor to come into your class, think not only about the benefit the visitor can bring to the class but what your pupils can do for the visitor. You will need to get the children to plan questions and so on but they should also plan what they are going to tell or show the visitor. For example, if a police officer visits they could show him or her the road safety posters that they have designed. If an elderly person comes to talk about life in the town when she or he was young, ask the children to tell him or her about what they have already found out about the period. This is usually much appreciated and may start an interesting conversation and useful lines of enquiry. Check what visitors the children have received previously and remember that parents and even school staff, from the headteacher to the cleaners, can be considered as potential visitors. It is good for the children to see these sorts of people in different capacities.

Display

Display is another area that will require planning. You need display for a variety of purposes, as you will be aware, but you should always ask yourself, *Do the children need this*? If the answer is 'No', then don't do it. Do not have a display just for the sake of it and everything you do display should be displayed properly. Set high standards for your classroom and

never tolerate a scrappy display; a bare wall is a better option. Always double-mount, always place things straight and use a little imagination. Ask a colleague's advice, or read a book on the subject if you feel that this is not your particular strength. Do not be less than competent – people will judge your class by its wrapping. Two small tips: always crop or trim work on a guillotine, especially artwork, even if you don't think that it needs it; and if you work to an outside border the interior of a display will usually take care of itself.

Where possible, try to have displays that represent the variety of work the children have undertaken. Don't just celebrate the fine artist or story writer; maths, science, RE and the other subjects all deserve attention. One advantage of having a range of subjects represented on your walls is that they provide evidence to the visitor (inspector or other) of the variety of work that you have been doing.

The teaching

When it comes to planning particular lessons, and the teaching that you will do, individual preference takes over. It is right that a variety of styles should flourish. You are an individual and when you teach you will be giving something of yourself to your class and they should benefit from your strengths. Nevertheless, you will be constrained by various legal requirements (dealing with a whole range of special needs and statemented children, for example); school and national policies; and pressures to work in some ways rather than others. A few things need to be clear. You should, over a period of a day rather than a week, use a balance of class, group and individual instruction. There is growing pressure (including the pressure of growing class size) to increase the proportion of class teaching. Generally, you will need to plan the lowest common denominator activity for the whole-class sessions. These will then lead on to group work, differentiated according to need. Here you should be looking to arrange for 'low guidance – high quality' activities for the more able children so that you will be able to visit and revisit those groups who need more help and repetition. When you have decided what it is you are going to teach, you must try to think up as many different ways of doing it as you can.

Children in the SEN register

The less able will need to use more than one of these ways: the more able will manage with fewer. Those children on the SEN register will require highly differentiated teaching. It will not be sufficient to differentiate by task; you will need to give them more time, more adult intervention, a greater range of apparatus, quality instruction and more success. Differentiate their work in as many ways as you can within the time available.

Defined lesson phases

Generalisations about teaching can result in banal statements that do not reflect the vitality, inspiration and sheer efficiency of a good teacher at work. But, running that risk, it can be said that a 'good' lesson has a beginning, a middle, and an end. If you think about what you are going to do in each of these three phases then you are on your way to success. It helps to make sure that the phases are clearly defined. Do not, for example, drift into a topic without having fully researched it; don't forget to have effective activities for the middle phase and do remember to bring the lesson to a satisfactory conclusion. While it will not always work this way in reality, this is a good method to aim towards.

Individual teaching and recording

The main problems with teaching plans for a Year 2 class centre on individual teaching and recording work. A seven-year-old still naturally demands a lot of individual attention but, when it comes to the teaching of reading and to making assessments, individual attention is essential on some occasions. Timetable when you intend to make time for individuals and make the children aware of this time so that they learn to respect the fact that 'It is Alice's time now' and know that they should not interrupt. The pressure to produce and retain evidence of children's work to support assessment judgements, justify report statements and satisfy the inspector, has led to an increase in the amount of recording that children now do. In Key Stage 1 the amount of recording used to be regarded as minimal but that is no longer the case, and in Year 2, the end of the key stage, the need for assessment demands more recording. Year 2s can be very slow recording tasks so you must allow time for this. Keep a camera ready to record evidence of work done which does not produce a clear written outcome.

Homework

Although they may not realise it, Key Stage 1 teachers have always been the most consistent providers of homework in the primary school. Reading books have always been sent home. The difference now is that you have to be more aware and organised about sending work home. Build it into your plans and records.

Your school may have a homework policy but the focus at this stage is bound to be on literacy and numeracy and, at Year 2, you should have SATs in mind. If possible, make an opportunity early in the year to talk to parents about homework, explain that it should be pressure-free and enjoyable. It should never become a battlefield. The vast majority of Year 2 children are eager to learn and to please their parents as well as their teacher and strife over homework should never be allowed to damage that eagerness.

Besides reading, the kind of things that you might expect children to do at home would be: practising number bonds; finding words that begin with particular sound blends; completing worksheets related to skills recently taught; and so on. Homework is no good unless it reaches home, so make 'homework bag check' part of your end-of-the-day routine.

Standard Assessment Tasks

Prepare for SATs from the beginning of the year. That is to say, spread your programme of work throughout the months leading up to the SATs in order to avoid panic. Even if you are experienced at SATs, it is still best to be prepared. Some teachers avoid using the word 'SATs' with children and use dummy-run testing under cover of 'testing the teaching'. You will need to make up your own mind about your method of approach. SATs have influenced the pattern of teaching in that they have shifted more emphasis onto the 'basics' (although that emphasis was already high) and they have altered some teaching strategies to fit what the tests demand. So a high concentration on language, particularly reading, and number work is the order of the day. Refer to some previous years' SAT papers and check what is expected. For example, if you use 'try spelling' books, you may have to modify your approach because children will need strategies that will carry them through the tests where 'try spelling' books cannot be used. You must give them strategies that can be used independently. Working towards becoming an independent speller might involve, for example, tapping

out the number of syllables and then trying to spell each syllable. Some teachers like to use 'magic lines' where the part the child feels confident with is spelt and a squiggle replaces the rest. These are the kind of variations that might arise from your assessment of your pupils' needs in relation to SATs. Assess where your pupils are as the year progresses to make sure that they are on course. Old SATs and commercially-produced materials are available if you need them. *Do they know their first 100 words?* (McNally) *The next 100? Do they know their number bonds to 10?* You may well wish to do exam-related activities. A good general rule is to focus on that which is abnormal in the SATs – seven-year-olds are not used to doing half hour tests, for example – and give the children some experience of it. Regular practice spread throughout the year is the best way forward, enabling the children to approach SATs confidently when they occur.

Teacher assessment

You need to make sure that your teacher assessments are geared to National Curriculum levels so familiarise yourself with them. Your school will probably have a moderation file with samples of work at each level for you to compare your judgements with, although there is no need to get worried about this. Level descriptors are very broad - most of your children will be Level 2, the bright Level 3, the others Level 1 with the poorer children at W. It is only at the margins between levels that you are likely to have any difficulty and, in any case, the judgement is not critical. Testing is carried out in May but you have the option to carry out reading tests earlier than this. **Do them as late as possible.** A child who is at Level 2A in January may be at Level 3 by May. If you have not been responsible for a SAT class before, talk to a colleague who has. SAT training courses are available and external moderators are usually extremely friendly and helpful. Keep all the paperwork and booklets filed and organised, there is a lot of it and you will not wish to get it into a muddle.

English
including Literacy Hour

This is an important year. Most of the children entering your class will have begun to read and write, and it is during this year that the acceleration in their literacy skills will begin to have dramatic effects on their oral ability. Until this age, children's skills in oracy will have been supporting their learning of reading and writing. This will continue to be the case, of course, but as confidence and fluency in reading increase, oral language will begin to benefit from the expanded range of vocabulary and syntactical patterns which are encountered in good children's literature.

However, those children who continue to have difficulty in reading will need special attention, as they may, during the course of this year, begin to see themselves as failures. Research has suggested that it is on the cusp between Key Stage 1 and Key Stage 2 that children begin to form firm perceptions of themselves as successful or unsuccessful learners, and hence their motivational patterns begin to establish themselves and to set the course for the rest of their school careers.

The National Curriculum suggests that the majority of children should be able to achieve around Level 2 during the course of this year. This means that they should be provided with opportunities to acquire and practise the following skills.

Speaking and listening

- Talking to a range of audiences (large and small, familiar and unfamiliar), about topics of personal interest. The degree of detail provided should show the beginnings of an awareness of the needs of different audiences.
- Speaking clearly, using appropriate vocabulary and intonation, to develop and explain ideas.
- Becoming aware of the occasions on which more formal vocabulary and tone of voice are used.
- Listening carefully to what others say in a range of situations (for example, storytime, assembly, discussion in a group or with another child or adult); demonstrating understanding and appreciation of what is said by making appropriate responses.

Reading

- Demonstrating comprehension of a range of texts, including stories, poems and non-fiction in print, reference and in ICT.
- Flexibly using phonic, graphic, syntactical and contextual clues to identify unfamiliar words in their reading.

Writing

- Communicating ideas clearly in several genres, including both narrative and non-narrative forms.

- Using interesting and appropriate vocabulary.
- Structuring sentences into coherent stories, reports and other compositions, demarcated with full stops and capital letters.
- Providing a degree of detail which takes into account the needs of the reader.
- Spelling common monosyllabic words correctly, and making plausible approximations to less common words.
- Forming both upper and lower case letters accurately, fluently and consistently.

Literacy Hour

The teaching framework devised by the National Literacy Project was the foundation for the literacy hour which was introduced into primary schools in September 1998. This one hour every day of dedicated teaching of reading and writing involves a rhythmic transition from whole-class teaching to small-group work and back again.

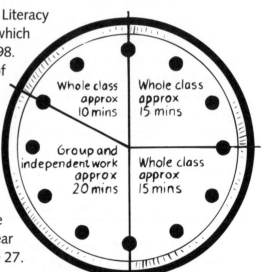

During this hour, children are engaged in work at whole text level involving comprehension and composition, work at sentence level involving grammar and punctuation, and work at word level involving vocabulary and spelling. Suggestions for the type of work that might be done at each level in Year 2 are outlined in the Practical ideas section on page 27.

What should they be able to do?
Key area: Speaking and listening

By the end of Year 2, the period of rapid language development that begins with the utterance of the child's first word, accelerates during the second and third years, and continues at a slower pace during the early school years is almost over, but this is not to say that language development is completed. Listening to six- and seven-year-olds talking, there is not a great deal of obvious structural difference between their language and that of adults. Most children of this age have a vocabulary of several thousand words. They can usually pronounce all the phonemes of English and are beginning to use complex sentences with an increasing degree of flexibility.

There are, however, many elements of English which children of this age have still to learn. The range of connecting words and phrases which children use to join up spoken sentences will have expanded somewhat beyond the repetitive use of *and*, which is characteristic of the speech of younger children, but will still be quite limited. Connectives like *however, for example, nevertheless, as a matter of fact, fortunately* or *in my opinion*, which help to give adult discourse its texture are very rare in the speech of Year 2 children. Children of this age are still sorting out differences between sets of words whose usage is related but distinct, such as *telling* somebody to do something, *asking* them to do it and *promising* them to do it. Many children will find difficult the use of some auxiliary verbs such as *may, might* and *ought to*. The over-generalised use of the -ed to mark the past tense of verbs, as in *sitted, thinked* and *runned* will be fading out of the speech of most

children, but will linger in some. Certain more complex sentence patterns, such as those containing a relative clause introduced by *whom* or *whose,* (for example, *The woman whose house we stayed in was weird*) are relatively rare.

Talking for everyday needs

In spite of these differences of detail between the speech of younger children and that of adults, it can be expected that all children who are speaking English as their first language will be able to use talk to indicate everyday needs. They should be able to relate personal experiences and talk about individual interests to a familiar audience, though the degree of enthusiasm with which they do this will, of course, vary from child to child.

Aim throughout the year to increase children's confidence by providing them with a variety of simple 'public speaking' opportunities, but it is important to respect the reticent child's right to a reasonable amount of silence. Regular participation in interactive story sessions should, by the end of the year, enable most of your class to tell or retell their own or a familiar story without the support of a book. Again, the degree of detail provided, and performance expertise displayed, will vary enormously. In both fictional and real-life recounts they should be able to identify and sequence the main points of the story that they are telling.

Sharing and extending learning through talk

Look for evidence that children are accustomed to using talk as a way of sharing and extending learning in several curricular areas. They should be able to talk about parts of books that they have found particularly interesting, discuss ways of approaching problem-solving tasks with other children, and be able to communicate any difficulties in understanding such tasks to you or their partners. They should also be able to recount what they have done in the course of the school day and indicate what they think they have learned from their activities.

Listening stamina

In the area of listening, a steady growth in 'listening stamina' should be evident throughout the year – provided, of course, that what the children are required to listen to is interesting and appropriate. This growth in attention span should be evident in an increased ability to do the following:
● Convey simple messages accurately and confidently;
● Follow a set of spoken instructions in the correct sequence;
● Respond to non-intrusive questions;
● Recall information from videos, books read aloud, and talks by other children and adults;
● Ask appropriate questions after they have been listening to such information (this, however, is quite an advanced skill, and you will need to demonstrate it for them throughout the year);
● Join in with the choral element in stories and songs;
● Speculate about the motives of characters in stories read aloud, and predict what is likely to happen next.

Knowledge about spoken language

As well as these uses of spoken language, children should, by the end of the year, be acquiring more detailed knowledge about spoken language. They should be aware that different levels of formality are appropriate to particular situations (the language used in talking about a holiday to your friends in the playground will differ from that used in describing

it at assembly). Listening activities, perhaps based on their own consumption of TV and radio, should have taught them something about regional, and age-based, variations in spoken language. (The concepts of accent and dialect are not too complex for children approaching the end of Key Stage 1.) Exploring these differences will provide a basis from which to build an understanding of standard English as the formal dialect.

Through poetry, song and wordplay, children should become aware of some of the phonological aspects of speech, such as *rhyme*, *rhythm*, *alliteration* and *onomatopoeia*, and how these are used for specific effects (for example, alliteration in tabloid headlines and advertising slogans; onomatopoeia in comics; rhyme in mnemonics and proverbs). Awareness of sounds within words, and of phonological relationships between words, will also help to improve children's skills in reading and writing.

Key area: Reading

The children in your Year 2 class will probably display a wide range of reading abilities which will be linked to varying levels of experience and enthusiasm. By the end of the year, some children will have become independent and omnivorous readers. Others, perhaps attracted by media more strident than print, or discouraged by the difficulties encountered in attaining literacy skills, may be struggling to maintain the competencies they brought with them from Year 1. The descriptions given below relate to what the National Curriculum guidelines refer to as 'the typical pupil', but bear in mind that such a thing is difficult to define.

The majority of children should be able to read simple narratives, poems and non-fiction texts independently, and be aware of the different purposes of these types of material and of the textual features which distinguish them. They should be able to show understanding of, and engagement in, their reading by making critical and appreciative comments while in conversation with you or with other children.

During the year, children should have been introduced to the use of non-fiction materials, including reference sources such as dictionaries and simple encyclopaedias. Many children will have learned how to use information texts to help them find answers to their own questions, and some will have started to become adept at using contents and index pages; all of your pupils should have at least some understanding of the purpose of these features. However, it is unlikely that the children will display as much skill in the use of non-fiction as they do in reading fiction.

By the end of the year, children should have extended their knowledge of traditional tales, including some from a range of cultures. They should also have read various stories by significant contemporary authors. During Year 2, many children are likely to begin forming opinions about their favourite authors and types of fiction. Encourage them to continue to read broadly, but allow them space and time to explore their more personal enthusiasms in greater depth.

Reading strategies

These general aspects of reading behaviour are underpinned by the increasingly flexible and rapid deployment of reading strategies. During Year 2, children who have begun to read will become increasingly aware of letter/sound relationships. Their ability to recognise whole words and analogies between onsets and rimes will continue to develop. By the end of the year, most children will probably be able to recognise several hundred words practically automatically, including high frequency words which are spelled irregularly, such as *because*, *wear*, *know*, *was*, *write*, *once*, *right*, *through*.

Writing tasks, in which they are required to build the spellings of the words they need to use, will result in a growing ability to separate phonemes in spoken words and to associate these with letters and with combinations of letters. By paying attention to environmental print, and by participating in shared writing sessions in which competent writers scribe for them, they will become aware of how consistent letter patterns reflect the sounds and meanings of words. While reading with adults or partners, they will develop the ability to identify unknown words by combining these phonic and graphic strategies with both grammatical knowledge *(What kind of word would make this sentence sound right?)* and contextual understanding *(What word would fit in with the meaning of what I've been reading?)*.

Co-ordinating all these sources of information can be difficult. You can expect that by the end of the year most children will, with the support of a competent reader, be able to deploy these strategies with some flexibility, but many children may still be relying too much on one preferred strategy. Typically, some children may work hard over sounding words out, while ignoring the syntactical and contextual (meaning) clues that would help them to identify unfamiliar words more quickly. Others rely too much on context and jump to conclusions about the identity of words without paying sufficient attention to the actual structure of the word. Your own example of how to co-ordinate strategies while you read with the child, and group activities involving different types of text completion, should help these problems.

Key area: Writing

Differing levels of achievement will also be apparent in the children's writing. The majority of children in your class should, by the end of the year, be confidently writing simple texts in narrative and non-narrative genres, supported by adequate groundwork and the use of prepared outlines and key vocabulary to ensure that these compositions are logically

organised. (See *Writing Frames* by Maureen Lewis and David Wray, RALIC.) By now they will have a stock of common or personally interesting words that they will be able to spell independently, and their growing awareness of letter/sound relationships will enable them to make phonic approximations to less familiar words. Children should be given the opportunity for regular handwriting practice, as well as everyday communicative writing tasks, as this should ensure that they are able to form both upper and lower case letters rapidly, easily and consistently.

Punctuation

Most children by now are likely to be using full stops and capital letters with some consistency, and more adventurous children may even be attempting to use other items of punctuation from their reading, such as speech marks, commas, question marks and exclamation marks. It is likely that all children will be better at identifying punctuation marks in reading than using them in writing. However, by the end of the year, the majority of the children should be confident enough to name the marks mentioned above and to understand what they are for.

However, a note of caution is necessary on this aspect of writing. Punctuation is based on both the grammatical and rhetorical aspects of language, and its use in published texts is frequently more flexible than rule-books suggest. Children tend more towards flexibility than rule-book rigidity when they are learning. For example, a child who writes: 'I wanted to jump off the slide. So I did. Straight away.' may not be conforming to rule-book usage, but she is making a skilled attempt to reflect the rhetoric of her thoughts as she writes, and is using the kind of staccato punctuation for effect that is often met with in published fiction and popular newspapers.

Understanding of sentence structure is also sometimes confused with the ability to punctuate conventionally; it is perfectly possible for children to construct quite sophisticated sentences before they have acquired a grasp of how to punctuate them. For example, a child who writes 'My dad came home from work fed up because they kicked him out of the job he had since he left school and its not fair' has not used a single punctuation mark, but he has managed to construct a sentence using a sophisticated assemblage of subordinated and co-ordinated clauses. Do not just focus on the surface errors, therefore, but remain aware of the strengths that children are capable of demonstrating in deeper aspects of language.

Non-fiction

As with reading, children will probably find writing in non-fiction forms more complex and demanding than story writing, though some children will be much more motivated to write about their real-life interests than to retell stories or to strive to produce fiction to order (the magnitude of this job is often underestimated by teachers).

Some children in your class may well be more advanced than this, emerging as competent and enthusiastic writers who enjoy and are capable of producing lengthy, complex and imaginative pieces of work. Other children, however, may be less confident. They may have anxieties about spelling, experience difficulties with the physical skill of handwriting, or have a simple antipathy towards the complex demands of this activity. It is important that you are perceptive to the needs of your pupils and design your programme of activities in such a way that the very different needs and requirements of both these sets of children are met.

Practical ideas

Making a start
Speaking and listening

Setting ground rules

While many children will come from their Year 1 class already accustomed to discussion activities and the type of considerate listening required, this will not always be the case, and it is generally a good idea to spend some time during the first days of term helping the children to set their own ground rules. Ask *What does a good talker do?* and *What does a good listener do?* Do not expect them to give fully-articulated and thought-through responses to these questions; that is why this is a good discussion activity. Most children, however, should be able to identify simple guidelines such as *Don't interrupt* and *Speak loud enough to be heard*, but some may decide that a good listener is one who never says anything, or a good talker is somebody who talks a lot. This would provide opportunities for broaching ideas like the need for the listener to provide encouragement and acknowledgement to the talker, and for the talker to be economical and relevant.

When some guidelines have been agreed, write them up as a classroom chart. This would make a valuable shared writing and reading activity for the early part of the school year, and the text produced can be used to monitor the quality of speaking and listening throughout the year. Some teachers have taped discussion sessions, then played parts of the tape back to the children for them to evaluate in the light of their own guidelines.

Pooling knowledge

What do we know? What are we learning? What have we discovered? When introducing new material in any subject area, it can be very useful to bring the children together and to ask them to pool all the knowledge that they already have about the area that you are going to explore, and then to brainstorm as many questions as possible about it. For example, if you've decided to take the origins of Bonfire Night as a topic in history, discussing the children's own experiences of this event will provide a motivating starting point, while their questions about it are more likely to steer their attention towards its origins and historical dimensions.

english

As the topic progresses, ask groups or individuals, at regular intervals, to give a spoken summary of what they have actually learned. At the end of the project, a whole-class session can be used for a final recapitulation of all that they have learned and done. This can then be turned into a written summary through shared or individual writing.

Developing key areas

Speaking and listening games

Most of the work done through oracy should occur as an integral part of regular lessons, but time should be found during the week for opportunities to develop speaking and listening in playful ways. Some traditional ideas are outlined below:

● **Travelling whispers:** a sentence is whispered to one child, who has to pass it on to another child, who passes it to a third, and so on until it has travelled all around the class. The sentence heard by the last child is then compared to the original sentence and, if necessary, some forensic examination work can be done on the changes that have occurred. In a more sophisticated version of this game, the first child is shown a picture or an unusual object, which he or she then has to describe to the next child.

● **Half a minute:** children select a topic which is of personal interest to them and talk about it to the rest of the class, or to a small group, for half a minute. If they hesitate, repeat themselves or deviate from the topic, a volunteer can then take up the thread and attempt to finish off the half minute talk.

● **Fortunately, unfortunately:** this game begins with a member of the group beginning a story with a sentence whose first word is *Fortunately*, the next person then has to continue the story with a sentence beginning with *Unfortunately*. The third person reverts to *fortunately*, and so on until the story is completed or breaks down. For example:
Fortunately, I managed to get up early for school this morning.
Unfortunately, I was in such a hurry I fell down the stairs.
Fortunately, there was a heap of cushions at the bottom of the stairs.

An elaboration of this game is for you to nominate connective words other than *fortunately* or *unfortunately* with which children have to continue the story. These might include *suddenly*, *sadly*, *however*, *in fact*, *eventually* and *at last*. Remember to demonstrate the use of these rather sophisticated constructions beforehand. These games tend to work better if you allow some turns to be taken without using a connective.

● **Sentence stretching:** this can be an entertaining way of learning about sentence structure and expansion. It begins with the first person saying a simple core sentence, for example:

The dog barked.

The next person then has to add a detail to the sentence to make it more informative or interesting.

The black dog barked.

The next person adds another detail.

The black dog barked loudly.

Players are also allowed to add phrases or clauses:

Yesterday morning, the black dog barked loudly.

Yesterday morning the black dog barked loudly when it felt the first shudder of the earthquake.

The sentence is passed around the group or the class with players adding words, phrases and clauses until it becomes too cumbersome to go any further.

● **Twenty questions:** one member of the group selects a person, object or idea as the subject (which might be related to a topic which is being studied or has been studied by the class). The rest of the group have to identify the person, object or idea by asking questions to which the leader can answer only 'Yes' or 'No'. If the idea has not been identified after 20 questions, the leader wins. Demonstrate how to ask effective questions and also how to 'recap' information given so far. A mathematical variation of this game limits the target idea to particular numbers.

● **In my grandmother's attic:** this game starts with a player saying 'In my grandmother's attic I found…' adding any object to complete the sentence. The second person repeats this then adds an object of their own. The game continues with the list of objects increasing each time. A monitor keeps a written list of the objects and disqualifies anybody who omits one. The game continues until the strain on the memory of the group is too great. A discussion on which objects are easiest to remember, and the strategies used by individuals for memorisation, can be interesting. A variant is that players supply objects whose names are in alphabetical order (I found an arrow, a broom, a comb, a doll…) – this makes more demands on invention but fewer on memorisation.

You can use some of these games to introduce writing activities and to teach grammatical terminology.

Using drama

Well-organised drama activities can contribute to social and language development in a number of ways. Co-operation, empathy and the use of collaborative talk can be furthered through situations in which children have to decide roles and purposes, organise material, consider audience needs and enter into the 'life spaces' of other people. As children work in role, they experience uses of language beyond those typical of the classroom, and may find opportunities to hear and use language patterns not normally encountered in their everyday repertoire. (It is important to note that drama here does not refer just to those scripted and staged performances that are eventually enacted in front of an audience.) The suggestions made below should give you some idea of the range of activities possible.

● Taking on roles to consider and 'play out' issues related to current concerns, for example taking the parts of a bully and his or her victim; parents discussing with a road safety officer their frustration at a ban on parking near the school; teachers discussing whether the proceeds of a car boot sale should be spent on books or sport equipment.

● Re-enacting historical occasions, customs, discoveries, disasters, and so on.

● Adopting the roles of characters in a story which has been read up to a certain point, then inventing different versions of how the story might develop.

● Examining current news stories and creating monologues or dialogues based on them. For example, the thoughts of an inhabitant of Montserrat contemplating the volcano; a conversation between a crew member on a stricken space station and his family on Earth.

● Taking fundamental themes from a well-known traditional story and adapting them through improvisation to a modern setting (for instance, the themes of being lost, imprisoned and triumphing over evil from *Hansel and Gretel*).

● Generating conversations based on 'What if…' situations. For example *What questions would we ask if somebody who knew everything visited the school? What if every pet in the world turned into a man-eater?*

The main learning potential for these activities comes in the thinking and talking that goes into the preparation of any eventual performance. Performance in the public sense should be regarded as an optional extra, though it does give children the opportunity to try to improve their voice skills.

Exploring language diversity

As mentioned in the introduction, children's familiarity with soap operas will provide a useful foundation for the discussion of how language varies regionally and internationally. Surveys and questionnaires can lead to discussion of the different languages and dialects that children or their families speak at home, though these need to be handled sensitively to ensure that parents are aware of the educational objectives of what might at first seem like intrusive or inappropriate inquiries. When you have the families' co-operation, interesting research can be done on age-related differences in language use, including changing fashions in slang and informal language. (Asking children to collect all the words and phrases that different generations have used for food, money and approval can be a fascinating starting point for talking about this.) Stories recited in a variety of languages and dialects can be tape-recorded to form a home-made local archive, and used for comparing regional dialects with standard English. Changes in the pronunciation and vocabulary of standard English itself can be investigated by viewing videos of news broadcasts and children's programmes from earlier decades (such as 'Andy Pandy'), and comparing them with current equivalents.

Storytime

The traditional fifteen or twenty minutes of storytime at the end of the day should be held sacrosanct as it provides hard-earned opportunities for relaxed and enjoyable listening. Diversify the types of listening that children engage in during this time by providing the following types of stimulus:

● Tapes of quiet or unusual music and other sounds that many children are unlikely to experience elsewhere.

● Encouraging children to tell or retell their own favourite stories (a tall story competition in which children are encouraged to invent the most outrageously improbable adventures for themselves and their friends and associates can work very well).

● Reading poetry and non-fiction as well as stories.

● Listening to story tapes, published and home-made, with and without sound effects, in order to broaden the range of voices that children hear.

● Listening to oral history tapes, in which people from a range of age-groups and backgrounds talk about their lives. A local library, museum or 'reminiscence centre' should be able to help with this, though organising the children to create a home-made archive of this type of material would be a valuable project.

Literacy Hour

The suggestions in this section have been organised in accordance with the *National Literacy Strategy* categories: work at word level (phonics, spelling and vocabulary); work at sentence level (grammar and punctuation), and work at text level (comprehension and composition). As in the case of speaking and listening, the two aspects of literacy have been dealt with together.

Text level work
From oral to written language

It will continue to be important to demonstrate with Year 2 children the basic idea that reading and writing are grounded in spoken language: that what they say can be written down and read back. This is a particularly important process to work through with less able readers and writers.

Accordingly, try to have regular sessions in which oral compositions are written down and 'published' via shared writing and word processing. This will enable children to see both the close links between talking and writing, and the crucial ways in which they differ. Some simple ways of organising this are suggested below:

● **Joke of the day:** This can be an enjoyable way of starting the day, and often allows less literary children an opportunity to acquire linguistic prestige. The joke is one of the most intense and economical forms of narrative, and the gradual composition of a class joke book, written 'in public' by the teacher as the joke teller talks, is one of the most effective ways of demonstrating the process of writing. A joke anthology can also be compiled on the computer using a multimedia authoring package which will enable you to file the jokes by type or under the name of the joke teller. Other forms of concise language play, such as tongue-twisters and riddles, can also be recorded in this way.

● **Tall tales:** The 'tall tales' activity suggested under 'Storytime' can form the raw material for a published collection of Baron Munchausen type stories. If the tall tales are told as part of storytime, it's a good idea to recall them a day or two later with the children and ask them to retell, embroider and dictate them to you or a helper for writing out and publishing.

● **Family episodes:** Children are usually ready to relate funny or dramatic episodes that have occurred in their families. Prompts such as the following will usually elicit something worth talking about and writing down: *What was the worst holiday that you have ever had? Has a member of your family ever tried to cook a meal and got it hopelessly wrong? Did your parents or grandparents ever get into trouble at school? What did your grandparents think of your parents' teenage tastes in clothing, music and hairstyles?*

From published writing to our own writing

As children's experiences of reading broaden, encourage them to reflect critically and appreciatively on what they have read by engaging them in occasional writing activities based on their reading. However, set such work cautiously and allow a degree of choice in the content. You do not want children to be put off their reading by marking each book read with a routine writing chore. The following suggestions may be offered as a set of possibilities from which children may select the most appealing:

● **Favourite character:** Provide a simple framework, using a worksheet or a computer-based outline, to enable children to make notes in the form of key words or phrases about their favourite character, and then to expand these notes into a connected description. Prompts can take the form of simple questions:

▶ *What is the character's name?*
▶ *What does she or he look like?*
▶ *What does she or he do in the stories you've read?*
▶ *Why do you like this character?*

Later, the same framework can be used to help children create their own characters.

● Other activities based on favourite characters might include, writing letters to the character, writing a new adventure for the character, or working on an interview in collaboration with a partner, in which each person takes it in turn to ask and answer questions.

● **Favourite places:** By the end of Year 2, some children may have become familiar with Narnia, Middle Earth or even Discworld (not necessarily through independent reading). Descriptive writing related to these fictional lands, based on the type of preparatory framework outlined above, can be augmented by more specific activities in which children might be asked to prepare a guide book, an annotated map or an illustrated flora and fauna for the chosen location. Again, at a later stage, children might be encouraged to invent their own fictional land.

● **Writing to the author:** A letter to the author of a personally-chosen book can make children more aware of the processes by which books are created, and provides a channel for expressing uncertainty and reservations as well as enthusiasm. It is essential that children write only to authors whose work they are both familiar with and feel strongly about. As a preliminary, write letters yourself to authors whose work you find interesting. Keep copies of both your original letters and any replies you receive, as these will provide both motivation and demonstrations.

Writing to a particular author could form part of the preparations for a book week featuring a visit by that author. Some children may want to write letters to authors who are no longer alive. The writing of such letters can help children to reflect more deeply on their reading. It can also lead to dramatic work in which children with a liking for a particular author work together to try to produce responses in role.

● **Castaway books, a database:** This idea might help to breathe fresh life into the potentially tedious business of producing book reviews.

Demonstrate the process by selecting three or four of your favourite children's books then, using a simple database such as *Grass* or *Claris Works*, record standard bibliographical information and a concise review focusing on what makes the book fascinating for you. (Some database programs allow the storage of 'free text' which will enable you to be discursive about this. Otherwise your 'review' will consist of key words and phrases.) Ask the children well in advance to start thinking about which five books they would most like to have with them if they were sent away to a distant planet. (They do not have to confine themselves to fiction.) As children make their nominations, demonstrate the use of the database and help them to enter their choices onto it. Explain that this is an open-ended activity, and once the planet books have been entered, they are free to add to the database throughout the year.

Cloze procedure

These are passages from which elements have been deleted. The children have to read the passages and use contextual clues to identify possible ways of restoring the deleted items. The nature of the deletions will depend on what skills you intend to develop. For example, restoring adverbs or adjectives might help to develop descriptive writing, restoring nouns related to a particular topic might reinforce the learning of specific vocabulary. Whole phrases can be deleted from sentences in order to encourage children to think about sentence structure, or particular letter strings can be removed in order for them to practise spelling patterns. Any well-designed cloze procedure involves a measure of comprehension, since the reader has to work from the overall meaning of the surrounding text to identify the missing element.

Cloze procedure can be a useful and enjoyable way of developing reading comprehension, but it is all too easy for it to degenerate into a routine, time-filling, gap-filling chore. The guidelines below should help you to avoid this.

▶ Make sure the content of the passages is relevant to the children's interests. It might be related to a topic that they are currently studying, or it might be taken from a summary of a book that they have recently read. Do not use disembodied chunks of irrelevant texts.

Once upon a time, a hungry fox was

prowling through a wood when he saw a

family enjoying a picnic. He decided to

creep up on them and _____ some

of their food. Just as he was about to leap

forward and snatch a pie, he _____

voices behind him. He _____

towards them and saw another family

having a _____ at the edge of the

wood.

▶ Cloze procedure should be done by pairs or small groups of children working together, so that the readers can compare their interpretations of what they have read and consider alternative ways of completing the passage.

▶ The task becomes frustrating if too many deletions are made. Always provide children with an intact introductory paragraph, and do not delete more than one word in ten. If you are working with phrases, keep at least one intact sentence between sentences which have had phrases deleted.

Appreciating poetry

Most children have an innate fascination with the rhythms and sonorities of poetic language, and an appreciation of alliteration and rhyme by children has been shown to be a reliable predictor of later reading ability. The activities outlined below are aimed at broadening children's knowledge of published poetry, helping them to become more aware of phonological and playful aspects of language, and encouraging them to experiment with these aspects themselves.

● Help the children to compile a classroom anthology. Begin it in September and expand it throughout the year. You can develop it in parallel versions in print, on audio tape, and electronically using a multimedia authoring package which might incorporate graphics and sound. Start with familiar forms like nursery rhymes and playground chants and songs, and move on to published poetry and the children's own compositions as the year progresses.

● Encourage the children to seek out, share and collect 'environmental' uses of alliteration, rhyme and word play in such places as newspaper headlines, graffiti, advertising and football chants.

● When focusing on specific phonic elements (for example, onsets like *scr-* and *thr-*, rimes like *-oom* and *-ight*), encourage children to make up alliterative sentences and stories, or lists of rhyming words that can be used to compose couplets or raps.

● Make a collection of nonsense poetry, share this with the children and encourage them to write their own. Present nonsense words from poems like 'Jabberwocky' and ask the children to speculate on their meanings. They can try to make up their own nonsense words, perhaps by making novel combinations of the phonic elements that they have been working with (for example, from above, scroom and thright), and can think about definitions for their new words.

Reading and writing non-fiction

Many Year 2 children will already have developed a preference for information books rather than fiction. To use these books effectively, they must:
▶ become familiar with conventions such as contents pages and indexes;
▶ acquire skills such as skimming and scanning;
▶ get used to bringing specific questions to the books;
▶ compare what they find with what they already know.

The programme of activities below is not meant to be exhaustive, but should help children to learn how these books might be used.

● **Sorting:** Prepare a number of sentences or short passages taken from stories, newspapers, dictionaries, information books and instructional texts such as recipe books and manuals. Ask groups of children to sort these into categories and to justify their choices. Focus on the extracts from information texts and help the children to identify what is distinctive about them.

● **Feature analysis:** Compile a collection of information books, at an appropriate level for the group you are working with, and a collection of stories. Mix them up and ask the children to sort them out. Work with the children to identify the features that distinguish a non-fiction book from a fiction one and discuss the function of each.

● **Generating questions:** This activity is linked with the 'Pooling knowledge' activity mentioned in the Speaking and listening section on page 27. Give the children a book related to the topic you are studying, ask them to pool their current knowledge about the topic, then to come up with questions to which they think the book might have the answers. These questions provide the starting point for you to demonstrate how to use the index and subheadings to search the text effectively for answers.

● **Underlining:** Prepare extracts from books at an appropriate level, each related to one of the questions that the children have already identified. Select one extract to enlarge to poster size and demonstrate to the children the process to be followed. Ask them to use the title of the extract to predict what it might be about and what might be learned from it. Read the text aloud with them, then re-read it, underlining words and phrases that relate to the question.

● **Tabulation:** Prepare a poster text related to a question that the class are investigating, and a table in which the categories can be used to summarise the information in the text. Read the text aloud with the children and demonstrate how words and phrases can be taken from the text and entered into the table. When this has been done, use the tabulated notes to compose with the children a summary of what has been learned from the text.

● **Pictorial representation:** This type of activity involves reading an extract from a book and using the information gained to draw a picture or to label a diagram.

● **Composing an information book:** This type of project occupies several sessions and is probably best left until the second or third term of Year 2, when children have developed their skills in using information books.

Decide on your own area of interest within a topic and prepare a mock-up of an information text related to that area. This should include all the features of a real information book, including a cover, information about the author, a glossary and a summary. Show this to the children and explain that this forms the framework for a book to be prepared over several weeks. Explain the choices you have made in identifying content, sequence of material, subheadings, illustrations and glossary entries.

The children can then work individually, in pairs or in groups, preparing their own mock-up books. Subsequent work throughout the term or half-term, incorporating a range of procedures for setting questions, note-making and reconstructing information from published books, will provide the eventual text for these books. Throughout this period, children can work co-operatively, commenting on each other's work and acting as proofreaders.

Instructional texts

Instructional texts are particularly valuable for young children because they are highly-structured, economical in their language, very closely related to things children can handle (such as tools, objects and ingredients) and because they create their own 'reward' for a successful reading in the form of the game that has been enjoyed, the toy that has been constructed, or the food that has been prepared.

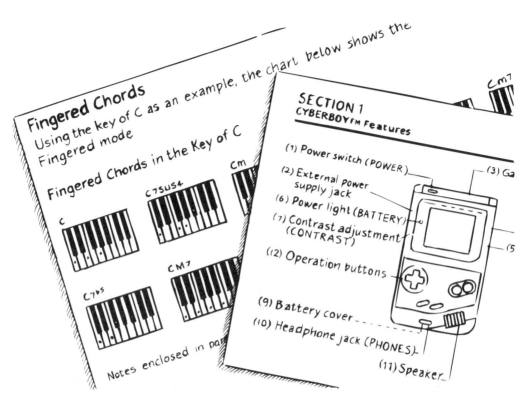

Investigation of these texts can be initiated by asking children to make a collection of them using sources such as the following:

▶ recipes from magazines, newspapers and food cartons;

▶ board and computer game instructions;

▶ instructions from DIY manuals, furniture kits and tool boxes.

The collection can be used to familiarise children with key features of the layout of such texts. Then, through shared or individual writing, children can create their own texts relevant to the classroom. These might include:

▶ instructions for using new computer programs, saving work on to disks and so on;

▶ tidying up routines;

▶ how to look after classroom plants or pets;

▶ procedures for setting up PE or science equipment safely.

Sentence level work

Avoid trying to explain what a sentence 'is'. There are over 200 available definitions, each of which is open to dispute. Rather than confusing children with various explanations, try to develop in them a feeling for the cadences of English: an intuitive sense of what sounds elegant and correct. In order to do this, wide reading and listening is essential. The first activity listed below encourages

children to focus on the structure and content of sentences in the course of such wide exposure to language patterns.

● **Make a sentence collection:** In the course of reading and listening activities, encourage children to identify and collect captivating beginnings to stories, effective concluding sentences, funny sayings, proverbs, notices, favourite lines of poetry and slogans. A focus on 'Sayings we love and hate' from home and school could be used to initiate this procedure. The items should be able to stand on their own as interesting examples of language, though whether they fulfil this condition or not will depend on individual tastes. The sentences can be used as raw material for any of the activities outlined below.

● **Sequencing, substitution, and slots:** Take any sentence related to a current concern and cut it into chunks based on phrase groups. For example: *Yesterday/we/planted/the sunflower seeds/in our garden.*

Mount the chunks on card and display them. Invite the children to experiment with ways of shuffling and resequencing the cards, seeing which reorganisations make sense and which don't. Then replace any of the chunks with a blank card, asking the children to suggest replacement phrases which could either preserve or alter the meaning of the original sentence. When substitutions don't work, ask the children to suggest further amendments which would rescue the 'rightness' of the sentence. For example, if a child suggested 'next year' as a substitute for 'yesterday' in the example, ask what else would have to be changed in the sentence for this to work. The children could also be encouraged to explore the possibilities of making incongruous substitutions. For example: *Yesterday/we/planted/pie and mash/in our garden.*

Sequencing and substituting can also be used with sentences which have been cut into separate words. Later, you can help children to identify 'slots' in sentences into which additional words and phrases can be introduced. For example;

1 The 2 sunflower 3 grew 4 quickly 5

1. last year
2. strongest
3. that we planted
4. very
5. because there was a ton of horse manure underneath it.

Activities like these can give children insights into sentence structure, but they need to be kept brisk, brief and frequent, and the sentences that you use should be as closely linked to the children's interests as possible. Linking these reading and writing activities to the oral games mentioned in the speaking and listening section on pages 27–30 can be particularly effective.

● **Sentence stems:** As well as providing practice in basic punctuation and sentence grammar, this set of activities can be used to help reluctant writers to commit themselves to paper by providing very simple frameworks for the expression of feelings.

Write up sentence stems such as the following on a shared writing board, or set them up as 'stationery' in a word processing program.
I get annoyed when...
I laugh when...
I wish that...

After discussion about how the stems might be finished, the children can complete them, using either shared or individual writing. Completions might consist of either single phrases or multiple alternatives. This procedure can be used with more competent readers and writers to develop more complex sentence structures.

_____ *is as annoying as* _____

Explaining things to my brother is as annoying as *losing my money on the way to the shops.*

We went to town and _____
We went to town but _____
We went to town because _____
We went to town until _____
We went to town although _____

Word level work

Collecting word families

Help children to make webs of words which are related in the following ways:

▶ By derivation, for example: night, nightmare, nightgown, tonight, goodnight;

▶ By association, for example: shout, scream, bawl, wail, howl, shriek;

▶ By opposition, for example: delightful/disgusting; dark/light; kind/cruel;

As well as expanding children's vocabularies and their knowledge of word structure, these collecting activities can be used to introduce them to the use of dictionaries and thesauruses.

Spoonerisms

Choose a common phrase, spoonerise it and invent a new meaning for it.
I'd like a cuff of copee, please.
He was eating chish and fips.
Get out your beading rooks and feading rolders.

ABCs

Children's knowledge of spelling, phonics and alphabetical order can be consolidated by activities in which they compose orally and then record in writing a variety of class alphabets: an alphabet of names; of real and imaginary animals; of favourite foods; of places; of books and story characters. Display the results as illustrated zigzag books or friezes.

Handwriting activities

The particular policy adopted by your school will determine the details of how you proceed in this, but it should be remembered that ten minutes of daily practice will do far more good than half an hour a week. During Year 2, children's enthusiasm for writing will show widening variations from child to child, and this will be reflected in the amount of stamina and commitment that they bring to this aspect of writing. Differentiated activities are therefore essential. There is no point in giving the same exercises both to children who can write fluently and to those who are still struggling with basic letter formation.

Some ways of encouraging children to focus on the formation of a limited set of target letters are outlined below.

● **Anagrams**
Select a word containing some letters that you want the children to practise. Ask them to find as many words as they can that can be made from the letters in the original word and to list them. Explore phenomena like perfect anagrams (vile, live, veil, evil; stop, pots, post, spot) as well as the more conventional, *How many words can you make from chrysanthemum?* type.

● **Palindromes**
Practise writing words and phrases that can be reversed: *dad, level, radar; Madam I'm Adam; Live not on evil*.

● **Caligrams**
Practise writing words so that the formation of the letters reflects the meaning of the word: fat, thin, and so on.

● **Pangrams**
Practise writing sentences in which each letter of the alphabet is represented. The most famous example is: *The quick brown fox jumped over the lazy dogs*, but children can be challenged to create their own.

Assessment

Speaking and listening

The important thing about assessing the oracy of young children is to defer judgement until you have compiled a record of the child's speaking and listening behaviour in various classroom situations and with a range of other speakers over the period of a term or more. Assessments based on anything less than this risk branding reticent children as 'language deficient', or judging children who merely talk a lot as being good talkers.

The absence of evidence of a looked-for capability on a particular occasion does not necessarily imply that capability does not exist. If children do not follow your instructions on a particular occasion, it could be that you have not expressed them clearly enough. A child's uncommunicativeness at school might be caused by shyness, language difference, or unfamiliarity with institutional norms, rather than by a lack of oral ability.

Informal, anecdotal and wide-ranging records of how a child talks and listens in a variety of classroom and other situations are essential, supplemented by what the child's family say about the child's speaking and listening outside school.

Many teachers find that the most convenient way of collecting such information is to have a notebook with a page or two dedicated to each child. This is left in a position where incidental observations, including verbatim snippets, can be jotted down by you and by classroom assistants. In order to build up a systematic picture, you could observe a small number of children each day. Over the course of time these observations can help you judge the children's progress in:

- communicating simple needs;
- participating in the recitation of repetitive patterns from stories and poems;
- responding personally to stories read aloud or shared with an adult during a reading conference;
- awareness of rhyme and alliteration;
- listening to, conveying and acting upon instructions;
- listening and responding to other children in group work;
- relating personal experiences and sharing personal interests;
- telling and retelling stories;
- asking questions about things that are difficult, interesting or puzzling.

Reading

Try to organise a reading conference with each new child as soon as possible after he or she starts in your class and make this as relaxed an occasion as possible. Physical comfort is essential and the book to be shared should be chosen by you and the child together. Aim to spend some of this time reading with the child, some of it listening to the child reading, and the rest of it talking about that particular book and about reading in general. As the child reads, make notes about the strategies being used (simple memorisation, attention to sound/spelling relationships, word length, pictures, context), and try to assess through discussion the child's appreciation and comprehension of the text.

After the initial conference, inexperienced readers should read with you, or with another competent reader, at least two or three times a week. Published recording systems such as

the Primary Language Record (CLPE 1988) and Progress in English (RALIC 1995) provide useful formats and detailed guidelines for the systematic reporting and interpretation of the information thus gained. Remember that this is a time not just for assessment, but for teaching children to apply what they have learned about context clues and sound/spelling relationships to the reading of their own books. It is also a time in which you can encourage children to make critical, personal responses to these books.

The reading conference is probably your richest source of data on the child's reading progress, but a fuller picture should also include elements such as reading diaries, in which you and the parents write to each other about what the child is reading, and reading strategies, records of the types of book and other material that the child has enjoyed, and information on the child's own view of him or herself as a reader.

In addition to this general information, many teachers also like to keep ticklist-type records in which the child's growing familiarity with particular phonic elements and items of sight vocabulary is monitored.

A cumulative record of the children's alphabetical knowledge (covering the names, sounds and formation of each letter) could be kept in this way, as could a record of their ability to recognise items from a list of high frequency words. (The National Literacy Strategy has produced suggested word-lists for each age-group.)

Writing

Much of what has been said about the assessment of reading also applies to writing. Observing children writing, and talking to them about their work, should help you to construct a picture of their skills and attitudes. Dated samples of writing of various types can be supported by observational notes about children's approach to the task, the level of help that they needed, and their own reflections on their work. The following points might help you to focus on important elements of the children's understanding of writing.

In writing or in talking about their writing, look for evidence that they can:
- produce and read back a coherent set of ideas;
- understand that changes can be made to a first draft;
- use a variety of forms of writing such as story, report of personal experience, letter, list of items for a particular job, and so on;
- use some vocabulary specifically related to the purpose of the writing (for example simple technical terms, or more 'literary' expressions in fiction);
- spell common words either correctly or in a phonically plausible way;
- make independent attempts at spelling unknown words by using word charts, dictionaries, and so on;
- form both upper and lower case letters legibly and with reasonable ease;
- locate letters on a keyboard with growing speed;
- use capital letters where appropriate;
- use full stops to demarcate sentences;
- appreciate that particular forms of writing (for example, recipes, personal letters, news reports) have distinctive layout features.

Mathematics
including Numeracy Hour

The teaching and learning opportunities that you provide your pupils with in Year 2 build upon the mathematical foundations established in their first years of schooling. It is on this base that all other pure mathematics (mathematical knowledge, skills and understanding) and applied mathematics (real-life, problem-solving investigations) are built in later years.

These experiences should allow children to begin to develop a firm understanding of mathematical concepts and make the necessary connections between:

mathematical symbols;
for example, '+' and '=' signs

mathematical language;
'plus', 'add', 'equals'

pictures; eg

and **concrete situations**. For instance, 'Five boys add three girls. How many children are there altogether?'

What follows should enable you to identify what stage in their development children are at now, and suggest how best to continue. It provides a scope and sequence for Year 2, with the focus on the learning objective rather than the activity, helping you to ensure progression and continuity.

Generally, children should be familiar and successful with the materials, language and activities for each learning objective before starting activities related to the following objective. Mathematics, however, is not a fixed, linear, hierarchical discipline: it is cumulative rather than sequential. Although the learning objectives in this chapter show a step-by-step sequence, the way you use them will depend on the appropriate needs, strengths and abilities of individual children.

Language

Children need to experience mathematics in a rich oral environment, for it is through language that they make meaning out of their experiences.

While you need to accept children's early mathematical vocabulary, you should help them to develop more formal mathematical language as it is required. For example, when learning about subtraction, children may use terms such as *take away* and *makes*. However, when you are discussing maths and talking to them, you can use terms such as *subtract*, *minus* and *equals*.

When children are asked to talk about what they are doing and thinking in mathematics they not only clarify and develop their own understanding but also articulate their level of understanding to others. It is important that they become good communicators of mathematics and can clarify observations and discoveries and convey their findings to others as they explore and investigate mathematics.

Ask children questions that will help them to:

● make connections in mathematics; for example, the link between the current teaching and learning objective and that of previous objectives. (*Do you remember our work on 3-D shapes that we carried out last week? How does that work help you to answer this question?*)

● develop a greater understanding of the learning objective; that is the link between the teaching and learning objective and the various mathematical activities. (*What have you learnt from the game you have just played?*)

● make new discoveries in mathematics; bring to their attention a new concept that is evident from the current teaching and learning objective. (*Can you tell me what have you done so far?*)

● apply their mathematical knowledge to other contexts; for example, money, shape, measures, other problems – (*If we know that 25 – 6 = 19, what do you think 25p – 6p equals?*)

Children new to English

Hindu	International
٩	1
₹	2
₃	3
४	4
५	5
६	6

There may be some children within your class for whom English is a second or other language. The ability of these children to communicate in English will vary considerably. This makes your job of ascertaining where they are in their mathematical understanding, and where to take them forward, all the more difficult. ESOL children need to be exposed to the English mathematical vocabulary and symbols as soon as possible. However, they first need to be able to make the connection between both the written and spoken mathematical language and symbols of their mother tongue with their English equivalent. You may find there are mathematical charts in community languages available in your area. If not, enlist the help of parents or older children who speak the language you need, to prepare charts with you.

Estimation and approximation

Provide children with plenty of opportunities to estimate a rough answer to a problem, and for them to approximate the range an answer is likely to occur within. This will help them to develop a 'feel' for numbers and assess whether an answer is reasonable or not. These skills also play an important role in their ability to measure with understanding. Real-life activities, such as cooking, sewing and building, help to develop their estimation and approximation skills.

As children develop, encourage them to estimate as close to the actual answer as possible in a variety of contexts, with a range of materials and units.

Linking concrete apparatus and mental mathematics

Children's first experiences of the world of mathematics should involve the use of concrete materials and real-life objects that are relevant and practical to their own experiences. They need to develop their initial understanding of mathematical concepts through the manipulation of everyday objects. This manipulation enables them to see and touch the mathematics they are engaging in.

There does, however, come a time when they are ready to move away from manipulating concrete apparatus and begin to internalise their understanding. This internalisation of the mathematics can be thought of as the initial stage of 'mental mathematics'.

Unfortunately children do not give off a signal when this internalisation has occurred and so it is difficult to know precisely when the need for concrete apparatus has passed. It is only through observation, questions and discussions that you can begin to ascertain whether they are ready to work without the apparatus. (*You have just shown me that if you have seventeen cubes and you take away four cubes you will have thirteen cubes left. Let's put the cubes away. Can you tell me what seventeen subtract four is?*)

There will, however, be times when children will need to return to using concrete apparatus and this should always be available for them to use whenever they want.

By the end of Year 2, most children should be able to recall certain mathematical facts from memory. For example, they should not only have an understanding of addition and subtraction facts to 10, but should also have instant recall of these facts. This recall enables them to quickly apply their mathematical knowledge of known facts (5 + 3 = 8) to unknown or 'derived' facts (so they can work out that 65 + 3 = 68).

Children's recording

When you introduce a new mathematics topic in Year 2 the emphasis should be on practical experiences and talking about mathematics. Children should not be required to write or copy copious amounts of mathematical calculations. However, by the end of Year 2 they should be able to record their results confidently, using both their own methods of recording and the more conventional mathematical recording techniques.

Numeracy Hour

It is currently recommended that at Key Stage 1 mathematics should be taught for 45 minutes every day. During the Numeracy Hour, all the children should be working on mathematics at the same time for the whole period. The mathematics you do in the Numeracy Hour will not be part of a general theme or integrated work but is focused on teaching specific mathematical concepts and methods.

You will be spending most of the time directly teaching and questioning the class. Children should spend approximately half of their time in a direct teaching relationship with you and the rest of the time working independently either in groups, pairs or individually. Each lesson should follow this structure.

Oral work and mental calculation (about 10 minutes).
Aimed at:
● developing mental fluency in previously taught concepts/methods and developing children's oral skills (whole class).

Main activity (about 25 minutes).
Aimed at:
● introducing children to new mathematical concepts/methods (whole class, group); or
● consolidating previously taught concepts/methods (whole class, group); and
● providing children with opportunities to practise, consolidate, use and apply taught mathematical concepts/methods (groups, pairs, individuals).

Plenary (about 10 minutes)
Aimed at drawing together the main teaching points of the lesson (whole class).

Many of the suggestions in the Practical ideas section of this chapter (see page 52) are suitable for using in the Numeracy Hour.

What should they be able to do?

Key area: Using and applying mathematics

When planning for Attainment Target 1 you need to provide children with opportunities to:
- use and apply mathematical knowledge, skills and understanding, that have been previously taught, practised and consolidated, in problem-solving situations;
- acquire knowledge, skills and understandings through 'real-life', meaningful, problem-solving investigations.

By the end of Year 2, children should have had appropriate and sufficient experiences that will help them in the following key areas. In all cases, the reference to 'children' refers to the majority of children.

Problem solving

Children should be able to:
- select and use materials appropriate for a particular task;
- select and use mathematics appropriate for a particular task;
- begin to develop their own strategies for working through a problem;
- begin to understand the ways of working through a problem;
- plan their work both mentally and using simple diagrams or pictures;
- check their work;
- complete a task.

Communicating

Children should be able to:
- make sense of a task;
- interpret mathematical information;
- talk about their work using familiar mathematical language;
- respond to and ask mathematical questions;
- represent their work using symbols and simple diagrams;
- choose their own method of recording.

Reasoning

Children should be able to:
- make and test simple predictions and statements;
- recognise and use simple patterns or relationships;
- make a simple generalisation;
- ask questions such as, *What would happen if...?, Why...?*
- begin to use logical thinking;
- begin to develop simple strategies.

Key area: Number

Children should be given opportunities to develop both their own and standard methods of working, mentally, orally and in the written form; in a variety of contexts, using a range of practical resources.

In order to ensure that children receive a broad and balanced range of experiences, you need to provide pupils with activities that employ the following tools:

- concrete materials;
- mental mathematics;
- paper and pencils;
- information and communication technology.

Numbers and the number system

Children should be able to:
- count forwards to 1000 and beyond;
- count backwards from 1000 and beyond;
- recognise, read, write and order numbers to 1000 and beyond;
- recognise written number names to 1000;
- count a given set of objects;
- make groups of objects of a specific size;
- understand that the position of a digit in a number represents its worth, eg 6 in 679 represents 6 hundreds;
- group objects to show the number of hundreds, tens and units;
- exchange objects up to 1000;
- recognise ordinal numbers;
- read a calculator display;
- begin to make sensible estimates and approximations;
- round a three-digit number to the nearest 10.

Money

Children should be able to:
- recognise all coins;
- use 1p, 2p, 5p, 10p, 20p coins in simple contexts;
- use combinations of coins to make amounts up to 20p;
- trade a number of 1p, 2p, 5p, 10p coins for a 20p coin;
- add and subtract amounts of money up to 20p;
- understand that 100p equals £1;
- recognise £ symbol.

Fractions

Children should be able to:
- divide an object into equal parts – halves and quarters;
- understand and use simple fractions of measurement, eg ½ teaspoon, ¼ past;
- recognise the equivalence between two familiar fractions;
- divide a set of objects into equal parts – halves and quarters.

Negative numbers

Children need to be able to appreciate the meaning of negative whole numbers in familiar contexts, for example, a temperature scale, a number line, a calculator display.

Patterns

Children should be able to:
- recognise patterns involving numbers to 1000;
- count forwards in ones, twos, fives and tens;
- count backwards in ones, twos, fives and tens;

- copy, continue and devise patterns involving numbers to 1000;
- recognise odd and even numbers;
- explore and use the patterns in addition and subtraction facts to 10;
- explore and use the patterns in multiplication and related division facts including 2×, 5×, 10×;
- make generalisations about patterns;
- make predictions about patterns;
- record observations.

Calculations

Addition

Children should be able to:
- understand and use the addition '+' and equals '=' signs;
- understand and use the vocabulary associated with addition, *add, plus, total, and, sum of, more than*;
- understand number patterns in addition facts to 10;
- recall basic addition number facts to 10;
- understand and use addition facts to 20;
- add three single-digit numbers mentally;
- add two two-digit numbers using appropriate apparatus;
- add two two-digit numbers mentally where the units do not cross the tens boundary.

Subtraction

Children should be able to:

● understand and use the subtraction '−' and equals '=' signs;

● understand and use the vocabulary associated with subtraction: *subtract, minus, take away, difference, less than*;

● understand number patterns in subtraction facts to 10;

● recall basic subtraction number facts to 10;

● understand and use subtraction facts to 20;

● subtract two two-digit numbers using appropriate apparatus;

● subtract two two-digit numbers mentally where the units do not cross the tens boundary.

Addition and subtraction

Children should be able to:

● understand the relationship between addition and subtraction;

● develop mental strategies for addition and subtraction;

● develop paper and pencil methods for calculations;

● solve problems involving known addition and subtraction facts;

● choose the appropriate operation when solving addition and subtraction problems.

Multiplication

Children should be able to:

● understand the concept of multiplication;

● understand and use the vocabulary associated with multiplication: *multiplication, multiply, times, lots of, groups of, sets of*;

● understand and use the multiplication '×' and equals '=' signs;

● develop an understanding of multiplication as repeated addition;

● know that $2 + 2 + 2 + 2$ is the same as 4×2;

● understand that multiplication can be done in any order, i.e. 3×2 is the same as 2×3;

● explore patterns leading to the creation of 2×, 5× and 10× multiplication tables;

● recall 2×, 5× and 10× multiplication tables.

Division

Children should be able to:

● understand the concept of division;

● understand and use the vocabulary associated with division: *division, divide, group, share*;

● understand and use the division '÷' and equals '=' signs;

● develop an understanding of partitioning (where the number of subsets is known), for instance share 20 sweets between 4 children;

● develop an understanding of repeated subtraction (where the number in each subset is known), eg if there are 20 sweets how many people would each receive 5 sweets?;

● develop an understanding of the division facts related to the 2×, 5× and 10× multiplication tables.

Multiplication and division

Children should be able to:

● understand the relationship between multiplication and division;

- develop mental strategies for multiplication and division;
- develop paper and pencil methods for calculations;
- solve problems involving known multiplication and division facts;
- choose the appropriate operation when solving multiplication and division problems.

Solving numerical problems

Children should be able to:
- solve numerical problems involving known addition, subtraction, multiplication and division facts in the context of real-life, investigative problems involving:
- money;
- length;
- mass;
- volume and capacity;
- time.

Processing, representing and interpreting data

Children should be able to:
- sort objects based on given criteria using a Venn Diagram;
- sort objects based on own criteria using a Venn Diagram;
- construct a block graph (where intervals increase by 1 or more);
- interpret a block graph;
- construct a pictogram (where one picture represents one or more items);
- interpret a pictogram.

Key area: Shape, space and measures

Children enter Year 2 with a practical understanding of their world gained through movement of themselves, interaction with others and with everyday objects around them.

In Attainment Target 3, activities involving concrete apparatus provide opportunities for allowing children to develop their spatial and geometric skills, knowledge and understanding.

Understanding patterns and properties of shape

Patterns

Children should be able to:
- copy, continue and devise a pattern;
- make generalisations about patterns;
- make predictions about patterns;
- record observations.

3-D Solids

Children should be able to:
- recognise and name a cube, cuboid, cylinder, and sphere;
- recognise and use appropriate vocabulary including faces, edges, vertices;
- describe the properties of 3-D solids;
- construct 3-D solids using various apparatus;
- sort known 3-D solids using a variety of criteria.

2-D Shapes

Children should be able to:
- recognise and name regular and irregular squares, rectangles, triangles, circles, hexagons and pentagons;
- recognise and use appropriate vocabulary including *sides*, *corners*;
- describe the properties of 2-D shapes;
- make 2-D shapes with increasing care and accuracy;
- sort known 2-D shapes using a variety of criteria.

Understanding properties of position and movement

Position

Children should continue to describe position and direction using appropriate vocabulary.

Movement

Children should be able to:
- recognise clockwise and anti-clockwise;
- understand movement in a straight line (translations);
- recognise whole, half and quarter turns (rotations);
- combine rotations and translations in simple ways.

Angle

Children should be able to:
- recognise right angles in shapes and in the environment;
- understand an angle as a measure of turn.

Symmetry

Children should be able to:
- make simple symmetrical patterns/pictures;
- recognise reflective symmetry in shapes and in the environment.

Understanding measures

Length

Children should be able to:
- recognise the centimetre length (cm);
- estimate and measure to the nearest centimetre;
- recognise the need for a unit larger than a centimetre;
- recognise the metre length (m);
- estimate and measure the length, height and distance of objects in metres and or centimetres;
- relate 100 centimetres to 1 metre;
- use measuring apparatus with increasing accuracy;
- record measurements.

Weight (Mass)[1]

Children should be able to:
- estimate and measure using the standard unit gram (g);

- recognise the need for a unit larger than a gram;
- estimate and measure using the standard unit kilogram (kg);
- use measuring apparatus with increasing accuracy;
- record measurements.

Volume and Capacity

Children should be able to:
- begin to use the litre as a standard unit (l);
- relate the litre to familiar everyday objects;
- estimate and measure to the nearest litre;
- recognise the need for a unit smaller than a litre;
- estimate and measure using half and quarter litres;
- use measuring apparatus with increasing accuracy;
- record measurements.

Time

Children should be able to:
- use a calendar to describe the days, weeks, months, seasons and years;
- tell the time of the hour on both digital and analogue clocks;
- tell the time of the half hour on both digital and analogue clocks;
- tell the time of the quarter hour on both digital and analogue clocks;
- calculate time intervals using both digital and analogue clocks.

---

[1] 'Weight', the amount of pull something exerts, is properly measured in newtons; 'mass', the amount of a substance, is measured in grams. However, in practice at Key Stage 1, it is acceptable to treat weight as synonymous with mass.

Practical ideas

Classroom organisation

The following practical ideas can be taught in different ways. Nearly all of them can be introduced to the whole class – perhaps with the children sitting round you. The children can then continue or complete the activity in groups. These can either be mixed or like-ability groups. You may want to offer extension ideas to groups who finish first.

Children can work on many of the activities that are suggested individually, but some of the activities, particularly games, are suitable for children working in pairs.

Making a start

The first activities under each main heading are particularly suitable for introducing the concept.

Assessment

Almost all of the activities can be used for some form of assessment. However, activities that have the symbol ✪ next to them are particularly suitable for assessment purposes.

Generally, there is progression within the group of activities under each main heading and so you may want to follow the sequence shown.

Using and applying mathematics

When you undertake a particular investigation with your class, you can base it on the particular mathematics topic you are concentrating on at that time, for example 3-D solids, length or time. This not only helps children to acquire new knowledge, skills and understanding but also to use and apply their existing knowledge, skills and understanding in a real-life, problem-solving investigation.

Numeracy Hour

Many of the practical ideas which follow are suitable for using in the Numeracy Hour. For example, if you were introduced to the concept of half of a group of objects, your numeracy hour could follow this pattern:

Oral work and mental calculation
▶ Count round the room in ones.
▶ Count round the room in ones. Children who say odd numbers have to put their left hands on their right ears (see page 57).
▶ Count round the room in twos.

Main activity
▶ Divide a group of six cubes in half (see page 56).
▶ Children complete worksheets (for instance, colour half the circles and so on)

Plenary (about 10 minutes)
▶ Ask individual children to share with the rest of the class what they have been doing.
▶ Discuss the main teaching points of the lesson.

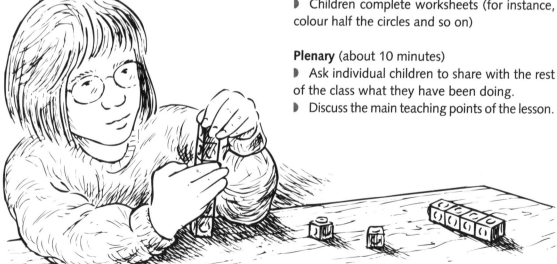

Number

Numbers and the number system

Knowing numbers

● ✪ Ask the children to count round the room within the range 0–1000, forwards and backwards. Start from any number. As you count around the room each child has to say the next number using a different voice, for example, softly, loudly, nervously, like a dog, and so on.

● Display number posters for numbers within the range 0–1000 to familiarise children with place value. On the number poster display the number, number name and when appropriate, a picture of a group of objects corresponding to the number.

For example:

253
two hundred and fifty three

● Children match a set of number cards and number name cards within the range 0–1000. For example:

four hundred and seven
407
two hundred and eighty two
282

Using 1–100 chart and squares

● ✪ Count forwards or backwards in ones. Ask children to identify the patterns that occur in the columns and rows. For instance, a pattern of 5s in the unit column, a pattern of 2s in the tens row. (See diagram below.)

● Ask children to finish off an incomplete 1–100 square. (See diagram on page 54.)
Variation: children can complete an incomplete 1–100 square which is laid out differently with the numerals running vertically in columns rather than in rows.

1	2	3	4	5	6	7	8	9	10
11	12	13	14	15	16	17	18	19	20
21	22	23	24	25	26	27	28	29	30
31	32	33	34	35	36	37	38	39	40

Mathematics

1	2		4	5	6	7		9	10
11	12	13		15	16	17	18	19	20
	22	23	24	25		27	28		30
31	32		34	35	36		38	39	40

1	11	21	31	41	51	61	71	81	91
2	12	22	32	42	52	62	72	82	92
3	13	23	33	43	53	63	73	83	93
4	14	24	34	44	54	64	74	84	94

● Cover up a number or numbers and ask the children to identify the ones you have covered.

● Give the children a 1–100 square jigsaw. Ask them to break it up and put it back together. Variation: children could make their own 1–100 square jigsaw.

● More able children can repeat the activities outlined above using a 1–1000 square and numbers within the range 0–1000.

Using a set of 0–100 cards

● ☺ Children can put:

▶ a pack of jumbled 0–100 cards in order;
▶ all the cards with: 1 unit in one pile;
   2 units in one pile;
   3 units in one pile, and so on;
▶ all the cards with: 1 ten in one pile;
   2 tens in one pile;
   3 tens in one pile, and so on;
▶ all the even numbers in one pile and the odd numbers in another pile.

Extend to include a selection of cards within the range 0–1000 and repeat the above activities.

● Deal out a jumbled set of 0–100 number cards. Ask two children to come out to the front and each display one of their number cards, for instance 46 and 67. Ask the other children to stand up if they have a number which is in between those two numbers. Repeat the activity, using different pairs of numbers.

● ☺ Matching game 0–100. Shuffle a selection of 0–100 number cards and corresponding number name cards together. Spread the cards face down on the table. Play Pelmanism (pairs) with them.
Variation: Use a selection of 0–1000 number cards and corresponding number name cards.

Tens and units

● ☺ Using Base 10 material, show, for example, 5 tens and 3 ones to the class. (If Base 10 material is not available, interlocking cubes can be made into towers of 10 to represent tens, and single cubes can be used to represent units.) Ask the children, *How many cubes do I have altogether?* Ask a child to answer by selecting the correct number cards and number name cards.

● Repeat, using other numbers to 1000, if you have Base 10 material. Show, for example, 618, using the number cards and ask a child to represent the same number using the Base 10 material. Children can work in pairs to continue the activity choosing numbers for each other.

● Display two numbers using Base 10 material and number cards, for example, 36 and 62. Ask: *Which number is larger/smaller? How can you tell?* Use other numbers such as 502 and 205, 741 and 471.

● ✪ Count forwards and backwards in multiples of 2, 5 and 10. Move on to using different starting numbers (66, 64, 62, 60, 58, 56… 93, 83, 73, and so on).

● Ask a child to make a tower of 24 interlocking cubes. Ask another child to add 10 cubes to the tower to make a tower of 34 interlocking cubes. Ask a third child to add another 10 cubes. *What does twenty four and ten make? What does thirty four and ten make?* Discuss the pattern, 24, 34, 44, …94.
Variation: with able children extend to include numbers within the range 0–1000, using Base 10 material and adding 100 each time.

● Display cards showing the multiples of 10. Remove a card and ask children to identify the missing number. Jumble the cards and ask the children to order them correctly.

Ordinal numbers

● Randomly hand out a series of ordinal cards and ask the children to arrange themselves in order.

● ✪ On occasions when the children are lined up, ask: *Who is fifth in line? Who is seventh from the end of the line? What position is Toby in the line?* and so on. During sports activities encourage children to identify their position in the group or their place in the game.

Using a calculator.

● After teacher demonstration, the children can carry out some of these activities.
▷ Encourage free play with the calculator.
▷ Enter your age/phone number/house number.
▷ Make number patterns on the calculator display.
▷ Make/draw calculator numbers.
▷ Solve a calculation.
▷ Type in the largest/smallest number using any three digits.

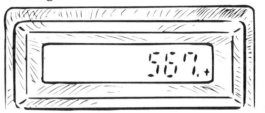

Estimation and approximation

● Encourage children to develop their estimation and approximation skills by asking them questions such as:
▷ *How many dots are on this page?*
▷ *How many letters are on this piece of newspaper?*
▷ *How many cubes are in this container?*
▷ *How many toes are there in the class?*
▷ *How many hours in a week?*
▷ *How many paces is it from the classroom to the school office?*
▷ *What is 567 + 345?*

● Show the children a number card in the range 0–1000 and ask them to round it to the nearest ten. For instance, 746 rounded to the nearest ten is 750.

Money

● Establish which children understand the value of all the coins. Arrange plenty of activities such as matching, sorting and ordering coins for those who are not so confident.

● Children can play 'shops' in groups. For the less confident groups, label a collection of shop items 1p, 2p, 5p, 10p, 20p. For more able groups label the items with prices involving combinations of coins up to 20p. Give the children purses with coins in them (1p, 2p, 5p, 10p, 20p). Children who are confident with money can have 50p and £1 coins and price labels for any price up to £5. One child in the group is the shopkeeper, the others are the shoppers.

The shoppers choose an item and offer the correct amount of money, using the fewest number of coins possible. The shopkeeper checks to see that the amount offered is correct before accepting the coins and handing over the purchase.

This activity can be extended for all groups by limiting the number of coin denominations so that the shopkeeper has to give change. Ask the children questions such as, *How much money is there in the till/in your purse?*

● ✪ Ask children to arrange combinations of coins to make amounts up to 20p. For example:
$5p + 2p + 2p + 2p = 11p$
$10p + 1p = 11p$
$5p + 5p + 1p = 11p$

● Encourage children to apply their knowledge of addition and subtraction number facts to solve calculations involving amounts of money up to 20p.

Fractions

● Hold up an apple, then cut it in half. Say to the class: *This apple has been cut into two parts. Each is the same size. Can anyone tell me what we call each part?* Write 'a half' and '$\frac{1}{2}$' on the board.

● Hold up each half of the apple then cut it in half. Say:*This half of the apple has been cut in half. Each of the four pieces is the same size. What do we call each part?* Write 'a quarter' and '$\frac{1}{4}$' on the board. Repeat using other objects, such as string, an orange, paper, material, a cake.

● Discuss the concept of a half and a quarter in relation to measurements, for example: $\frac{1}{2}$ a teaspoon of coffee, $\frac{1}{2}$ a mug of milk, $\frac{1}{4}$ past 3.

● Count out six cubes. Say to the children: *I am going to divide these six cubes into two halves. I am going to share them evenly between Sam and Imogen.*

Give out the cubes alternately, one to each child, and ask *How many cubes does each child have?* Say: *One half of six is three.* Write '$\frac{1}{2}$ of 6 = 3' on the board. Repeat using different objects, such as counters and marbles, and the numbers, 8, 10, 14.

● Count out eight pencils. Say to the class: *I am going to share them evenly between four people: Bethan, Michael, Chung and Gita.* Give out the pencils, one to each child in turn. *How many pencils does each child have?* Explain to the children, *One quarter of eight is two.* Write '$\frac{1}{4}$ of 8 = 2' on the board. Repeat using other objects and numbers, such as 12, 16, 20.

● ✪ Ask children to divide a set of objects, such as cubes, into halves and quarters and to write down the corresponding calculation.

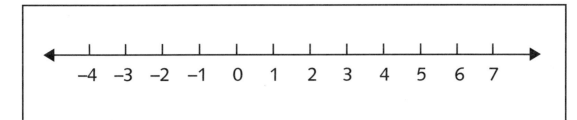

Negative numbers

● Introduce the concept of negative numbers using a number line. Discuss the fact that numbers go on forever in both directions, hence the arrows on the number line. (See diagram above.)

● Play 'Reach minus one'. Each child has a number line and a counter and chooses where to place his or her counter on the number line (any number except 0). Throw a dice. Before you call out the number thrown, say either *add* or *subtract*. Children then have to move their counter along the corresponding number of spaces in the right direction. Keep throwing the dice and calling out *add* or *subtract* until a child lands on –1.

● Discuss with the children the concept of negative numbers in familiar contexts such as a thermometer or on a calculator display.

Patterns

● Use a 1–100 chart to identify the patterns that occur in the columns and rows.

● Ask the children to count forwards and backwards in ones, twos, fives and tens.

● Identify the patterns in addition and subtraction number facts to 10.

● Identify the patterns in 2×, 5×, 10× multiplication and related division facts.

0 + 6 = 6	6 – 6 = 0
1 + 5 = 6	6 – 5 = 1
2 + 4 = 6	6 – 4 = 2
3 + 3 = 6	6 – 3 = 3
4 + 2 = 6	6 – 2 = 4
5 + 1 = 6	6 – 1 = 5
6 + 0 = 6	6 – 0 = 6

1 x 2 = 2	2 ÷ 2 = 1
2 x 2 = 4	4 ÷ 2 = 2
3 x 2 = 6	6 ÷ 2 = 3
4 x 2 = 8	8 ÷ 2 = 4
5 x 2 = 10	10 ÷ 2 = 5
6 x 2 = 12	12 ÷ 2 = 6

Recognising odd and even numbers

● Children count round the room. If they call out an even number they must put their hands on their head. (Alternatively, they could cross their arms, kneel, and so on.)

● Ask children to sort a shuffled pack of 0–100 or a random selection of 0–1000 cards into odds and evens.

● Ask the children to find numbers in the environment. *Are they odd or even?*

Calculations

Addition
Mental strategies

Children often find crossing the ten boundary difficult, (for example 5 + 7 =, 6 + 4 + 7 =). Teach them a range of mental strategies to help them to solve these types of calculations easily. For example:

▶ start with the largest number first;

▶ count forward in repeated steps (ones, twos, threes);

▶ know that 6 + 5 is the same as 5 + 6;

▶ use two stages to add 9 (+ 10 – 1);

▶ use two stages to add 11 or 12 (+ 10 + 1 or + 10 + 2);

▶ know doubles, eg 6 + 6;

▶ use near doubles, based on doubles already known, e.g. 6 + 7 is one more than 6 + 6;

‣ partition 6, 7, 8 or 9 into '5 and something'

9 + 7

(5 + 4) + (5 + 2)

(5 + 5) + (4 + 2)

10 + 6 = 16;

‣ partition into '10 and something',

15 + 14

(10 + 10) + (5 + 4)

20 + 9 = 29;

‣ increase the largest number to the next multiple of 10 and add the remainder,

8 + 5 =

(8 + 2) + 3 =

Apparatus

A number of teaching methods, using appropriate apparatus, can be used to show children addition number statements involving:

‣ addition facts to 20;

‣ addition of three single-digit numbers;

‣ addition of two two-digit numbers;

‣ addition of two two-digit numbers mentally where the units do not cross the ten boundary. Some of these methods include the use of the following apparatus.

Dice

● Using two dice, children take turns to throw the dice, add the numbers together and write down the corresponding addition number statement and answer.

Variation: Use three dice.

● Throw a dice and call out the number of dots on it, for instance three. Ask the children to make ten from that number. Children write down the answer which when added to three equals ten, so that in this example the answer would be seven.

Variation: Make other numbers to 20. Throw two dice. The children add them together, then work out what needs to be added to the total to make 20.

Interlocking cubes

● Place seven cubes in a feely bag, then add another six. *How many are there altogether in the bag?* Repeat, using different combinations of cubes up to a total of 20.

● Use two different colours to demonstrate addition number facts for 3, 4, 5, 6, 7, 8, 9, 10. An example of addition number facts for 8 is given below.

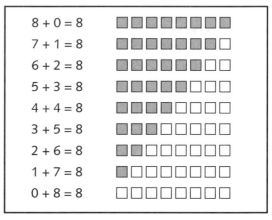

| 8 + 0 = 8 |
| 7 + 1 = 8 |
| 6 + 2 = 8 |
| 5 + 3 = 8 |
| 4 + 4 = 8 |
| 3 + 5 = 8 |
| 2 + 6 = 8 |
| 1 + 7 = 8 |
| 0 + 8 = 8 |

● Use three different colours to demonstrate addition of three single digit numbers. For example, 5 + 3 + 6 =

● Use a grid of 20 squares positioned into two rows of 10 squares to demonstrate addition number facts between 10 and 20. This will involve answers that cross the ten boundary. (See below.)

7 + 5 =

(7 + 3) + 2 =

10 + 2 =

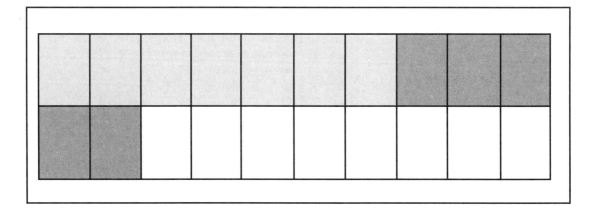

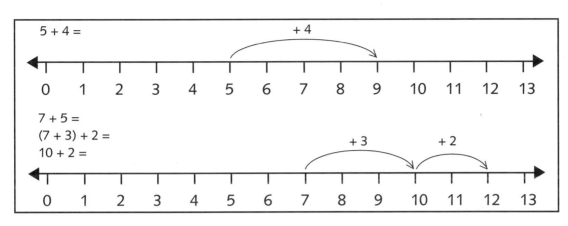

Number line

Use the number line to show the children how to regroup numbers that cross the ten boundary.

Base 10 material

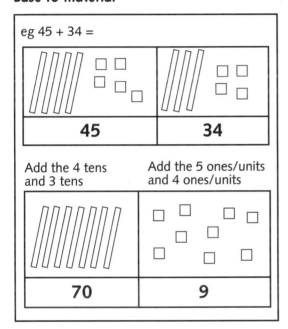

Subtraction

Mental strategies

Teach the children a range of mental strategies that will help them to solve subtraction calculations easily. For example:

▶ count backwards in repeated steps;

▶ explain that, if we know that $6 + 5 = 11$, then we also know what $11 - 5$ and $11 - 6$ are, as all three calculations involve the same three numbers (5, 6, 11);

▶ use two stages to subtract 9 ($- 10 + 1$);

▶ use two stages to subtract 11 ($- 10 - 1$);

▶ decrease the largest number to the next multiple of 10 and subtract the remainder, for example, $14 - 6 = (14 - 4) - 2 = 10 - 2 =$

Apparatus

A number of teaching methods, using appropriate apparatus, can be used to show children subtraction number statements involving:

▶ subtraction facts to 20;

▶ subtraction of two two-digit numbers;

▶ subtraction of two two-digit numbers mentally where the units do not cross the ten boundary.

Some of these methods include the use of the following apparatus.

Dice

● Using two dice, children take turns to throw the dice and subtract the smaller number from the larger number. They then write down the corresponding subtraction number statement with the answer.

● Throw a dice and call out the number of dots on it. Ask the children to subtract that number from ten and write down the answer.

Variation: Subtract from 7, 8, 9, 11 up to 20.

Cubes

● Place 13 cubes in a feely bag, take out four and ask: *How many are left in the bag?* Repeat using up to 20 cubes.

● Use towers of cubes to demonstrate subtraction number facts for 3, 4, 5, 6, 7, 8, 9, 10. For example, subtraction number facts for 7 could look like this.

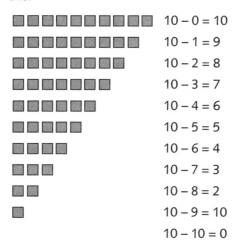

7 – 0 = 7
7 – 1 = 6 (remove 1 cube)
7 – 2 = 5 (remove 2 cubes)
7 – 3 = 4 (remove 3 cubes)
7 – 4 = 3 (remove 4 cubes)
7 – 5 = 2 (remove 5 cubes)
7 – 6 = 1 (remove 6 cubes)
7 – 7 = 0 (remove 7 cubes)

Subtraction number facts for 10 could look like this.

10 – 0 = 10
10 – 1 = 9
10 – 2 = 8
10 – 3 = 7
10 – 4 = 6
10 – 5 = 5
10 – 6 = 4
10 – 7 = 3
10 – 8 = 2
10 – 9 = 10
10 – 10 = 0

Number line

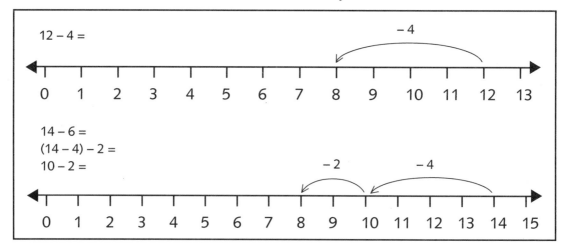

12 – 4 =

14 – 6 =
(14 – 4) – 2 =
10 – 2 =

Base 10 material

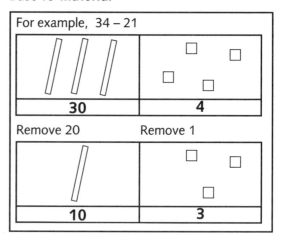

For example, 34 – 21

30	4

Remove 20   Remove 1

10	3

Number families

Addition and subtraction numbers facts to ten can both be taught together using the notion of number families.
For example, the number families for six:

0, 6, 6	1, 5, 6	2, 4, 6	3, 3, 6
0 + 6 =	1 + 5 =	2 + 4 =	3 + 3 =
6 + 0 =	5 + 1 =	4 + 2 =	6 – 3 =
6 – 0 =	6 – 1 =	6 – 2 =	
6 – 6 =	6 – 5 =	6 – 4 =	

Inverse relationship

● Teach the children the notion of the inverse relationship between subtraction and addition.
For example: 4 + 3 = 7   3 + 4 = 7
7 – 4 = 3   7 – 3 = 4

Introducing multiplication

● Count around the classroom in two fives and tens. Use a number line or 1–100 chart if necessary.

● Give five children a tower of ten cubes each. Ask each child to count the number of cubes they have. Together, count the total number of cubes in multiples of ten – *10, 20, 30, 40, 50*. Ask: *How many towers are there? How many are there in each tower?* Write 10 + 10 + 10 + 10 + 10 = 50 on the board and say: *There are five lots of ten. There are fifty cubes altogether.*

Show the children the multiplication sign (×). Write 5 × 10 = 50 on the board. Repeat, using different numbers of children with ten-cube towers. Demonstrate the multiplication sentence but omit the repeated addition stage.

● Repeat the same process as above to develop an understanding of the multiplication facts for 2× and 5×.

● Use other appropriate apparatus for the 10× tables such as Base 10 equipment, buttons, counters, children.

● Introduce the vocabulary associated with multiplication: *multiplication, multiply, times, groups of, lots of, sets of.*

Introducing division

● Count out 30 counters in front of the class and say: *We are going to share these thirty counters evenly among ten children.* Choose ten children and give one counter to each of them, then another, and so on. Ask the children, *How many counters do each of you have?* They will answer 3. Explain to the class, *Thirty shared among ten is three.* Write on the board 30 ÷ 10 = 3. Repeat, using counters in different multiples of ten.

● Repeat the same process as above to develop an understanding of the division facts related to the 2× and 5× multiplication tables, using counters in multiples of two and five.

● Identify the patterns in 2×, 5×, 10× multiplication and related division facts.
For example:

1 × 2 = 2	2 ÷ 2 = 1
2 × 2 = 4	4 ÷ 2 = 2
3 × 2 = 6	6 ÷ 2 = 3
4 × 2 = 8	8 ÷ 2 = 4
5 × 2 = 10	10 ÷ 2 = 5
6 × 2 = 12	12 ÷ 2 = 6

Inverse relationships
● Teach the children the notion of the inverse relationships between division and multiplication.

For example: 4 × 5 = 20   5 × 4 = 20
20 ÷ 4 = 5   20 ÷ 5 = 4

Consolidating understanding of the four rules
● Have a wall chart displaying addition, subtraction, multiplication and division number facts.

$$7 - 0 = 7$$
$$7 - 1 = 6$$
$$7 - 2 = 5$$
$$7 - 3 = 4$$
$$7 - 4 = 3$$
$$7 - 5 = 2$$
$$7 - 6 = 1$$
$$7 - 7 = 0$$

● ✪ Ask children to show examples of addition, subtraction, multiplication or division facts using real objects.

● Play Addition Bingo with the class (addition number facts to 20). Ask children to write down any 16 numbers from 0 to 20 on a 4 × 4 grid.

● Give them number statements in the following ways:

▶ a number card, for example, 3 + 5 =

▶ throw two or three dice, call out the numbers on the dice and ask the children to add the numbers together;

▶ say an addition statement, for instance *Five add eight equals...*;

▶ use a problem-solving context, for example *Michael had 12p and was given another 5p. How much money did he have altogether?*

Children work out the answer. If they have that answer on their grid they cross out the number. Four crossed-out numbers in a line, vertically, horizontally or diagonally, means Bingo! Repeat until there is a winner with all the numbers on the grid crossed out.

Variations:

▶ Ask questions that involve the addition of three single-digit numbers using a 4 × 4 grid and numbers 0 to 27.

▶ For less able children, ask questions that involve addition number facts to 10 using a 3 × 3 grid and the numbers 0 to 10.

▶ For more able children, ask questions that involve the addition of two two-digit numbers mentally (where the units do not cross the 10 boundary) using a 5 × 5 grid and numbers 0–100.

▶ Play Bingo again, this time using subtraction and multiplication.

● ✪ Ask the children, *How many ways can you make seven?* (Or any number to 20). Some children may suggest simple additions and subtractions. More able children may devise more complex calculations involving all four rules and can move on to using larger numbers.

● ✪ Use flash cards with addition, subtraction, multiplication or division number facts to produce instant recall of number facts.

● ✪ Ask children to write examples of addition, subtraction, multiplication or division facts in real contexts.

I had 17 sweets. During the day I gave 3 to Tony, 4 to Daniel and 2 to Claire. By the end of the day I had 8 sweets left.

● Have a 'number of the day'. At various times during the day, ask a child to give a number statement for that day's number using any operation or computational method they can.

● Continually encourage children to describe their mental methods of calculation.

Solving numerical problems

Children should have experiences of applying their knowledge of number in a variety of contexts, including:

◗ money;
◗ length;
◗ mass;
◗ volume and capacity;
◗ time.

Processing, representing and interpreting data

Non-intersecting circles

● Ask the children to sort objects using two non-intersecting circles (hoops, string or circles drawn on a large sheet of paper). Criteria might include:

◗ is a cylinder/is not a cylinder;
◗ an object you use in the kitchen/an object you use in the bathroom;
◗ is a fruit/is a vegetable;
◗ can bend/cannot bend.

Children sort objects or pictures into the appropriate circles. If objects do not fit into either circle, they remain outside both of them.

● Repeat the activity using hoops or rope rings and the children themselves. Criteria might include: sex, hair colour, length of hair, eye colour, type of shoes, colour of clothes.

Intersecting circles

● Prepare some number cards from 1–6. Choose six children and ask each of them to pick a number card.

Children then sort themselves using two intersecting circles (hoops, string or circles drawn on a large sheet of paper) labelled in various ways. For instance, 'Numbers less than 4' and 'Numbers between 2 and 6'. Discuss what happens to the child who has the number three. Agree that he or she should stand in the intersection of both circles.

● Repeat the activity using number cards from 1–10 and smaller circles drawn on paper to put just the cards in. Children can work in ability groups and you can give them labels of appropriate difficulty. For example, able children could be given labels such as:

◗ 'Odd numbers' and 'More than 6' (8 and 10 go in the intersection, 4 and 2 are outside the circles);
◗ 'Less than 4' and 'Even numbers' (2 goes in the intersection, 5, 7 and 9 are outside the circles) Children can write their own labels for friends to work with.

Less able groups can work with non-intersecting circles and simple labels ('1 to 5' and 'More than 5') until they are confident.

Block graphs and pictographs

● Draw a blank block graph on a large sheet of paper.

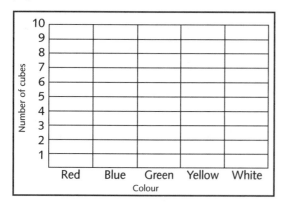

● Ask each child to pick a cube from a bag which contains a quantity of cubes in the five different colours on the graph. Ask one child to say the colour of his or her cube. All the other children with that colour then stand up. Together count the standing children. A child can colour the corresponding number of squares on the block graph while the activity is repeated for the other colours.

When the block graph is completed, ask questions that will enable the children to interpret the graph: *How many red/blue cubes are there? Which colour did we pick the most/least? Which colour was chosen five times?*

● Repeat the activity above. However, this time the intervals on the graph increase by more than one.

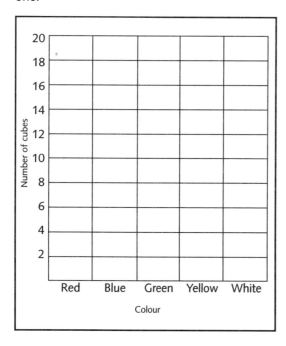

● ✪ Encourage children to make their own block graphs (where the intervals increase by one or more) collecting other information, such as favourite game, number of siblings, shoe size, and so on.

● Draw a pictograph on a large sheet of paper.

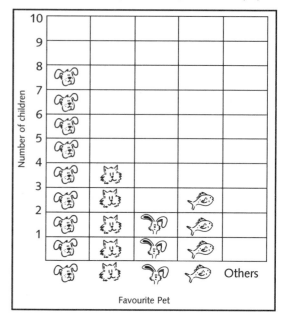

Ask each child to name which of the pets on the pictogram is their favourite. Make a tally on the board for each pet to keep a record of the number of votes.

● Discuss with the children the concept of a tally. Continue the activity as for the block graph activity – drawing pictures to show the tally for each of the pets. When the pictograph is completed, ask questions that will enable the children to interpret the graph: *How many dogs are there? Which animal is our favourite/least favourite? Which animal did six people choose as their favourite?*

● Repeat the activity above. However, this time the intervals increase by more than one.

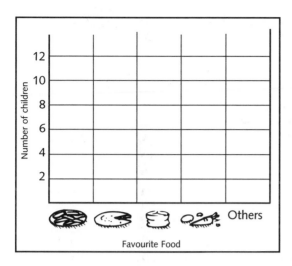

● ✪ Children can make their own pictographs (where the intervals increase by one or more) using other information, such as 'Favourite colour', 'How I get to school'.

Information and Communication Technology
● ✪ Children create simple block graphs and pictographs using a simple database package.

Shape, space and measures

Understanding patterns and properties of shape

Patterns
● ✪ Individually, children copy and continue patterns using different attributes, such as size, colour and shape.

● ✪ Children then devise their own patterns using different attributes. *Can your friend guess what will come next in the pattern?*

● ✪ Use a variety of objects to devise, copy and continue patterns. These could include interlocking cubes, attribute blocks, shapes, counters, commercially available pattern games, and everyday objects such as shells, pasta, pencils.

● Encourage children to record their patterns.

3-D shapes
● Show children a cube. Ask them to name and label it with you. Discuss its properties in relation to faces, edges and vertices. Repeat this for a cuboid, cylinder and sphere.

● ✪ Ask children to identify cubes, cuboids, cylinders and spheres in pictures, drawings and in the environment. Allow them to make posters such as 'Our cylinder collection' on which they can stick appropriate pictures they have found. Alternatively, or in addition, they could set up a display of real objects.

● ✪ Place a variety of 3-D solids in a feely bag. Ask individual children to choose a shape and describe it while it is still in the bag. Encourage them to talk about its faces, edges and vertices. The rest of the class have to try and identify the shape. The child then pulls the shape out to see if the class were correct and places the shape beside an appropriate label.

● ✪ What am I? A child describes the attributes of a shape or object and the class have to try and identify what it is from memory.

● Provide a selection of boxes of various shapes and sizes. Ask the children to pull them apart and reassemble them.
Variation: Children can trace around the net of the boxes on to thin card, cut around the net and assemble the shape.

● Get children to construct 3-D solids using various construction materials, including paper.

● ✪ Ask children to sort a collection of 3-D solids and everyday objects according to faces, edges and vertices.

2-D shapes
● Draw a square on the board or on a large sheet of paper. Name and label it with the class. Discuss its properties in relation to sides and corners. Repeat this for regular and irregular squares, rectangles, triangles, circles, hexagons and pentagons.

● ✪ See if children can identify regular and irregular squares, rectangles, triangles, circles, hexagons and pentagons in pictures, drawings and in the environment. They can go on to make posters and displays.

● Matching game. Playing in pairs, children shuffle a variety of 2-D shape cards together (such as four lots of regular and irregular squares*, rectangles, triangles, circles, hexagons and pentagons) and play Pelmanism with them.

Variation: Provide six picture cards showing different regular shapes (for instance square, rectangle, triangle, circle, hexagon and pentagon) and six picture cards showing different irregular versions of the same shape. There are 12 label cards (one for each different shape but not labelled regular or irregular.) The child turns up two cards. If he gets a picture and a matching label they are a pair and he keeps them.

(*Squares and circles do not, strictly speaking, have irregular forms but, to children, a square on its point, or an oval are irregular.)

● ✪ Children sort a collection of 2-D shapes (regular and irregular) according to faces and corners.

Position and movement
Position

Discuss simple vocabulary to describe the position of an object and encourage the children to use it:

▶ in relation to themselves;
▶ in relation to other subjects;
▶ in describing models, pictures and diagrams.

Words could include *near, close, far, to the left, to the right, in front of, behind, beside, next, next to, above, across, along, around, after, back-to-back, before, behind, beside, top, bottom, centre, close, down, up, far, forward, further, from, here, high, low, in, inside, into, first, last, middle, near, on, onto, on top of, outside, over, past, right over, around, round, side by side, there, through, top, turn, under, over, underneath, up, upside down.*

● ✪ Children draw a sketch of an object (a toy a doll, an open book on its end, a LEGO model) on the table in front of them. Ask them to imagine that they are standing behind/to the left of/to the right of the model and to draw another picture from that position. They then go and stand in the suggested position and check their drawing.

● Play 'Copy my model'. Organise the children into pairs. Give each child LEGO bricks of the same colours and sizes. The children sit back to back and one child makes a LEGO model. He/she describes the model to the other child who has to try and make an exact copy without looking. They compare models and discuss the similarities and differences. They then reverse roles and repeat the activity.

Information and Communication Technology
● Use a Roamer/Turtle/Logo package to show position.

Movement
● During a PE session, ask the children to make straight and turning movements. Use a percussion instrument to signal changes in movement. Ask children to work together in pairs to form sequences that involve straight and turning movements.

● Use a clock face to introduce the notion of clockwise and anti-clockwise. Then follow this up in a PE session. The children can stand in two circles holding hands, one circle inside the other. Give directions for each circle to move clockwise or anti-clockwise. Start slowly, then increase the pace at which they move and the frequency with which they have to change direction.

Translation
● Introduce translation (movement in a straight line) by asking children to trace round a shape on to a sheet of paper. They then slide the shape along and draw around it again, repeat this to make a sequence of shapes and colour their sequence to make a pattern.
Variation: Use two shapes.

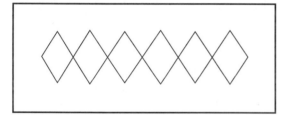

Rotation
● Introduce rotation (movement in whole, half and quarter turns) by asking the children to trace round a card or paper triangle. (Use a drawing pin to secure the triangle to a piece of paper on top of a board.) They then rotate the triangle a little, draw around it again and repeat. Once they understand this process, introduce the notion of whole, half and quarter turns and ask them to repeat the exercise using whole, half and quarter turns. Repeat using different shapes to create a range of different patterns.

● Collect fabric, wallpaper and wrapping paper designs with rotating and translating patterns. Discuss them and create a display.

● ☼ Children combine translations and rotations to create their own patterns.

Information and Communication Technology
Use a Roamer/Turtle/Logo package to draw various movement patterns.

Angle
Right angles
● Introduce the concept of a right angle by making right-angle testers. Give each child a sheet of paper. Ask them to fold the sheet of paper in half, then in half again. Explain that the corner measures a 'square corner'. Ask the children to draw a small square in the corner of their sheet of paper.

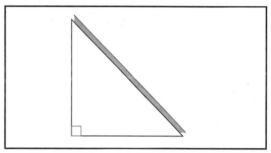

● Ask children to go around the classroom and use their tester to check for square corners, for example the corner of the blackboard, desk, book, door, bookcase.

● Introduce the terms *angle* and *right angle*. Explain to the children that the two edges of the door meet at an *angle* at the corner. If it is a square corner it is called a *right angle*.

Other angles
● Ask the children to find angles which are not right angles. For instance, between a sloping ceiling and wall, between the blades of a pair of scissors, where two fingers meet. (You can demonstrate smaller, right and larger angles by gradually opening the covers of a book.)

● ☼ Children find angles that are 'right angles' and those that are 'not right angles'. Ask: *Which angles are smaller than a right angle? Which angles are larger than a right angle?*

Symmetry
● Introduce the concept of symmetry by showing the children how they can make symmetrical patterns or pictures.

● Fold a piece of paper in half, draw a shape around the fold and cut out the shape.

● Fold and cut paper to make a snowflake.

● Fold a sheet of paper in half. Paint a simple picture on one half, then fold the sheet in half again so that the paint smudges.

● Look at the examples and discuss how the fold line divides the shape into two parts and how the two parts are the same – they are halves. Explain that shapes of this kind have *symmetry*. They are called *symmetrical shapes* and the fold line is called the *line of symmetry*.

● ✪ Children now make their own symmetrical shapes/patterns and then find examples of reflective symmetry in the environment.

Understanding measures

Length

● Ask the children to do some measuring with non-standard units (such as hand spans). Discuss with them the problems of measuring with non-standard units and the need for a standard unit of measurement. Introduce the ruler and the centimetre (cm) length.

● ✪ Working in pairs, children measure the length and height of or distance between various objects or people in and around the classroom using a centimetre ruler. Encourage them to:

▶ find objects of specific lengths, (for example,

an object that measures approximately 14cm);

▶ estimate the length of objects before measuring them;

▶ record both their estimates and actual measurements.

Discuss with them:

▶ the differences between their estimates and actual measurements;

▶ the concept of rounding measurements to the nearest centimetre.

● Discuss with the class the best way of measuring the length of the classroom using a centimetre ruler. Ask them to estimate, then choose two children to measure. Discuss with the children the differences between their estimates and the actual measurements and the difficulty of measuring such a large distance with a centimetre ruler. *Is there another way to measure the room?*

● Introduce the metre ruler and metre length (m). Relate 100 centimetres to 1 metre.

● ✪ Working in pairs, children measure the length and height of or distance between various objects or people in and around the classroom using both centimetre and metre rulers. Encourage them to;

▶ find objects of specific lengths, for instance you could stipulate that they must find something approximately 1m long;

▶ estimate the length of objects before measuring them;

▶ record both their estimates and actual measurements;

▶ choose the appropriate measure to work with;

▶ use measuring apparatus with increasing accuracy.

● Discuss with the children:

▶ the differences between their estimates and the actual measurements;

▶ the concept of rounding measurements to the nearest metre.

● Ask children to make lists of objects that are:

▶ less than a centimetre;

▶ exactly a centimetre;

▶ more than a centimetre but less than a metre;

▶ exactly a metre;

▶ more than a metre.

Weight (Mass)

Grams

● Discuss with the children the problems of weighing with non-standard units and using simple comparative language. Talk about the need for a standard unit of measurement. Introduce the standard measure, gram, and explain that we write it 'g'.

● Introduce the children to the 10g, 50g, 100g, 200g, and 500g masses. Discuss and compare them. Using the 10g mass and a balance, ask the children to estimate, then measure, how many beads, cubes, spoons of rice, and so on it will take to balance the mass. Record their estimates and measurements. Repeat using other masses.

● ✪ Using 10g, 50g, and 100g masses, children find items which weigh approximately the same. Encourage children to estimate first and to record both their estimates and actual measurements.

● ✪ Children choose individual small items and find out how much they weigh. Encourage children to use a variety of masses and combine them to ensure the most accurate measurement. Estimate first and record both their estimates and actual measurements.

● Encourage children to use a variety of weighing apparatus, for example, balances, scales, dial scales.

Kilograms

● Discuss with the children the difficulty in measuring heavy items in grams. Show the children the kilogram mass and introduce them to the standard measure, kilogram. Explain that we write this as 'kg'.

● Using the kilogram mass and a balance, ask the children to estimate, then measure, how many beads, scoops of rice or sand, marbles, and so on it will take to balance. Record their estimates and measurements.

● Children use smaller masses to balance a kilogram. Encourage children to think of different combinations of gram masses that will equal a kilogram mass.

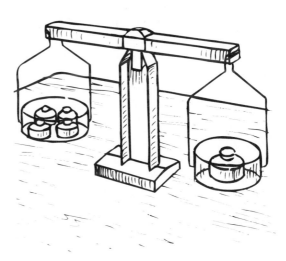

● ✪ Organise the children into pairs and ask them to weigh various objects in and around the classroom using both grams and kilograms. Encourage them to:
❱ find objects of specific mass, for example they must find something that weighs approximately 1kg and 50g;
❱ estimate the mass of objects before weighing them;
❱ record both their estimates and actual measurements;
❱ use measuring apparatus with increasing accuracy.
Discuss with the children the differences between their estimates and actual measurements

● Encourage children to find and make lists of objects that are exactly or approximately 10g/ 50g/100g/a kilogram/more than a kilogram.

Volume and Capacity

Capacity – the amount of space something will hold.

Litre

● Show the children a large container and a cup. Say to them, *We are going to see how much water this container will hold. We'll use this cup to measure. How many cups of water do you think the container will hold?* Record their estimates on the board then measure the container using cups of water. Write the actual measurement on the board. Discuss the differences between the children's estimates and the actual measurement. The children then repeat the activity using different measures, a yoghurt pot, margarine container, and so on.

● Discuss with them the difficulty of using different-sized measures and how it is easier if everyone uses the same measure. Introduce the standard measure, the litre. Explain that when using this measurement 'l' is written for short.

● Show the children a collection of litre containers.

● Display a collection of containers larger than a litre. Pick one and ask, *How many litres do you think this container will hold?* Record the children's estimates. Fill the litre measure and pour it into the container. Continue until the container is full, counting with the children the number of litres used. Record the answers. Discuss the differences between the children's estimates and the actual measurement.

● ✪ Working in pairs, children estimate and record how many litre measures will be needed to fill various containers. They then test and record the actual measurements.

● Encourage them to find other containers that hold exactly or approximately one litre.

Half and quarter litres

● Discuss with the children the problems of finding the capacity of containers that are smaller than a litre and the need for a unit smaller than a litre. Introduce the half litre measure. *How many half litres will it take to fill the litre measure?* Give the children some time to experiment with the half litre and litre measures and containers. Introduce the quarter litre measure in the same way. *How many quarter litres will it take to fill the litre measure? The half litre measure?*

● Show the children a collection of containers smaller than a litre and ask them, *How many half or quarter litres do you think this container will hold?* Record their estimates. Fill the container with water and pour it into the half or quarter litre measures. Record the actual measurement. Discuss the differences between the children's estimates and the actual measurement. Repeat the exercise using other containers.

● Some children may be ready to discuss the calibrations on the litre measure which show 1000 millilitres. Explain how the half litre is 500 millilitres and the quarter litre is 250 millilitres.

● ✪ Working in pairs children estimate how many half and quarter litres various containers hold. They record their estimates and actual measurements. Some children may be ready to estimate and record in millilitres.

● Ask children to make list of containers that hold:

◗ exactly a litre;
◗ more than a litre;
◗ half a litre;
◗ quarter of a litre.

Volume

Volume – the measurement of space in a solid shape.

● Using boxes and containers of various sizes, children estimate and count how many cubes/beads/counters/marbles, and so on will fit into the boxes and containers. They record their estimates and actual measurements.

● ✪ Encourage children to make models using various materials – unifix, LEGO, wooden blocks – and to count the number of blocks used.

✪ Children make different models using the same number of blocks.

Time

Use a calendar to consolidate children's understanding of the days of the week, months of the year, seasons and years.

Days

● Discuss the days of the week. Write down certain events that take place each day of the week in school.

● ✪ Ask children to create their own weekly diary of things that happen at home.

Months, seasons and years

● Discuss the names of the months, the weekly cycle, the number of days in each month. Record on a class-made calendar:

▶ special national events;
▶ special school events;
▶ special celebrations;
▶ birthdays of children in the class.

● Teach the children the rhyme *30 Days Has September* if they do not already know it and use it for handwriting practice. Create a big wall chart with the rhyme as centrepiece and decorate it with seasonal artwork.

● Teach the children the 'knuckle' calendar. The months on the bumps have 31 days, the months in the hollows (except February) have 30 days.

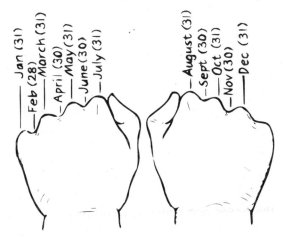

● Using seasonal pictures relate the four seasons to the calendar: when they occur, the differences between the seasons and things that occur in different seasons.

● Discuss the current year and previous years. Write down special events that have occurred:

▶ this year (*This is our last year in the infants*);
▶ last year (*Last year we had Mrs Miller as our teacher*);
▶ within the children's lifetime (*Adib's little sister was born in 1994*).

Write down special events that are likely to occur next year. (*Next year our class will be going swimming.*)

Telling the time

● Show the children an **analogue clock** and discuss clocks generally.

▶ Count the numbers.
▶ Talk about the hands on a clock.
▶ Introduce 'o'clock'.
▶ Talk about important times of the day that feature 'o'clock'.

Ask the children to draw pictures for these times of the day. Alongside, they draw the hands on a stamped clock face to show the time and write the time in words, for example '9 o'clock'. Repeat if necessary.

● Show the children a **digital clock**. Talk with the children about there being 60 minutes in an hour. Show the time on the hour using digital time.

● Introduce the term *half past*. Show the children an analogue clock displaying 3 o'clock. Move the minute hand to the 6 and explain to them *This is half past three. It is half way round the clock.*

Write the time on the board in both analogue (half past three, ½ past 3), and digital (3:30) time. Explain to the children that there are 30 minutes in half an hour, ½ × 60.

Repeat for other times and ask children to demonstrate some half hour times.

● Introduce a quarter past (*The minute hand is a **quarter** of the way past the hour*) and a quarter to (*The minute hand has travelled one quarter, two quarters, three quarters past four; the minute hand is at a **quarter** to the hour of five*) in the same way.

● ✪ Using analogue and digital clocks, show the children times (o'clock, half past, quarter to and quarter past) and ask them what time it is. Ask children to show particular times on the clocks.

● ✪ Set the time on a clock hidden from the children, give clues, for instance: *It is 15 minutes before 5 o'clock.* Children have to guess the time on the clock. They can repeat this activity in pairs.

● ✪ Children make their own digital and analogue clocks and use them to show various times (o'clock, half past, quarter to and quarter past). Children can take turns at testing each other's knowledge of times.

● ✪ Play a time-matching game. Working in pairs, children shuffle together two different sets of time cards and spread them face down on the table and play Pelmanism (pairs) with them.

Time keepers

In the classroom have:

▶ a calendar board with velcro-backed changeable dates, days and months;

▶ a large analogue clock positioned where everyone can see it and, if possible, a large digital clock, too.

▶ Appoint pairs of time keepers (match capable timekeepers with less confident ones) whose job is to update the board and, when appealed to at odd moments, announce the analogue or digital time.

Time intervals

● Using an analogue clock, show children the time on the clock and write the time on the board. Show children another time on the clock and write this time on the board.

Discuss with the children the time interval between the two times. Repeat the exercise. Carry out the activity using digital time.

At appropiate times during the day, give them opportunities for working out time intervals using o'clock, half past, quarter to and quarter past. (*You started painting at a quarter to three. What is the time now? How long have you been painting?*)

Assessment

Children demonstrate the outcomes of their learning through speaking, writing, drawing and engaging in other activities.

A variety of assessment strategies is necessary if you are to have an understanding of where your pupils are at in their learning and how best to further develop that understanding. Whatever assessment strategies you use, it is important to ensure that tasks are appropriate to the individual child and that they are directly related to the learning objectives. Remember that those activities marked with an ✪ in the Practical ideas section are suitable assessment activities.

The levels of expectation suggested at the beginning of this chapter under the 'What should they be able to do?' heading provide a comprehensive checklist for assessing your pupil's learning at the end of Key Stage 1.

Science

Although the National Curriculum specifies what science must be taught at Key Stage 1, each school has to decide in which order it should be taught and make some choices. The Orders for Key Stage 1 are divided up into a number of units of work to be taught over a six-term period. It is not practical to deal here with every possible combination of units, so the following programme for Year 2 is suggested.

	Autumn Term	Spring Term	Summer Term
Year 2	**Unit 3** *Materials and their Properties* **1.** Grouping materials **Unit 5** **1.** Electricity	**Unit 7** *Physical Processes* **3.** Light and sound	**Unit 1** *Life Processes and Living Things* **1.** Life processes **2.** Green plants as organisms **5.** Living things in the environment

(If your school has allocated the units differently, you may want to draw on the ideas in the Year 1 book where Units 2, 4 and 6 are covered.)

This programme ensures that in each year every child will cover work within all three of the knowledge and understanding Attainment Targets.

Unit 3, Grouping materials, was chosen as a starting point because it provides a number of opportunities for simple introductory investigations. The maverick unit is Unit 5, Electricity. This has been suggested as a follow-up to Unit 3 in the Autumn Term. This is partly because of the length of that term and also because one way of grouping materials is on the basis of whether or not they conduct electricity. Since Unit 5 does not readily lend itself to many truly scientific investigations, some teachers may prefer to teach it within Design and Technology activities. These two units contain a substantial amount of work and, therefore, may need the longer Autumn Term for their completion.

Unit 7, Light and sound, is a relatively small unit which will fit comfortably into what is often the very short Spring Term.

Unit 1 also contains a heavy workload. It concerns life processes, plant growth and natural habitats and ideally needs to be undertaken in the Summer Term to allow for outdoor work.

What should they be able to do?

The statutory Orders for Science are set down in four sections. When these are examined, it is easy to be lulled into believing that the three sections dealing with knowledge and understanding – *Life processes and living things*, *Materials and their properties* and *Physical processes* – put the emphasis on the content of science rather than the process. This notion is soon dispelled by the realisation that *Scientific enquiry (Sc1)* is regarded as having roughly equal importance to the other three science sections combined. Although it offers no facts to be learnt, Sc1 will only be achieved over a period of time, perhaps the whole of the primary school stage, or even longer. The aim is for children to develop an understanding of scientific phenomena through systematic and practical exploration and investigations.

The National Curriculum identifies three components within scientific investigations. They are: Planning, Obtaining and presenting evidence and Considering evidence and evaluating.

Planning

Young children have enquiring minds and are curious about everything around them. It comes naturally for them to try things out, to see how things work, to manipulate, to feel, to be curious, to ask questions and seek answers – exactly the attributes of a good scientist.

Planning includes asking questions and predicting. In this connection, it is important to provide plenty of opportunities that promote discussion between the children and between you and the children. The children should be encouraged to ask questions of the *Who? What? Where? When? Why? How many? How much? How far?* variety. Children will not automatically suggest ideas that can be investigated without prior practice but, towards the end of Year 2, they should be having opportunities to identify questions that can be investigated and to plan and carry out their own investigations which they have considered to ensure that they are fair. Most of these  investigations will be concerned with familiar, everyday experiences, but some will relate to contexts beyond their immediate experience, such as testing materials to see which would make the best damp-proof course for a house.

In Year 2, most children should be able to explain what a prediction is and how it differs from a guess. With continued practice in carrying out appropriate investigations, activities and discussion, they will acquire a basic scientific knowledge, and learn to make predictions that are based on both this knowledge and the data they have collected.

Obtaining and presenting evidence

Children should be encouraged to use all their senses to measure and record accurately. Year 2 children should be suggesting what observations can be made and suitable ways of measuring these. They should be recording their predictions and actual results, perhaps using a three- or four-column table.

Considering evidence and evaluating

This includes the interpretation of the results of their investigation and evaluating the scientific evidence. They should be encouraged to make comparisons, to look for patterns and to communicate their findings in a variety of ways. This gives them a great opportunity to share their thinking and to relate their understanding to scientific knowledge. In Year 2 most children's consideration of evidence will be limited to presenting findings in simple ways through talking and presenting and interpreting charts, tables, pictograms and simple bar charts. They should be able to provide explanations that relate to their knowledge of science in certain familiar contexts. They should also be able to suggest improvements to investigations, including ways of making an investigation fairer.

Knowledge and understanding

The three sections of the Programme of Study dealing with knowledge and understanding are *Sc2: Life processes and living things*; *Sc3: Materials and their properties*; and *Sc4: Physical processes*. These are instantly recognisable as the biology, chemistry and physics of secondary school days. Remember that the Programmes of Study are not always intended to show progression, and the letters a, b, c, and so on, do not always imply increasing complexity. It is also important to remember that the three Programmes of Study cannot be considered independently of *Sc1: Scientific enquiry*.

Breadth of study

Sc0 has now been incorporated into SC1 and the Breadth of study. This has consequences for investigative science, the process skills involved and subsequently planning and assessment. Children also need to be taught through science how major scientific ideas contribute to technological change – impacting on industry, business and medicine and improving quality of life; as well as knowing the cultural significance of science and tracing its worldwide development. They need to have the opportunity to learn to question and discuss science-based issues that may affect their own lives, the direction of society and the future of the world.

Practical ideas

🌀 Making a start

There are many ways of introducing the four units suggested for Year 2. The following are some suggestions. Others are suggested in the Ideas bank on page 88.

Grouping materials

● Collect together a variety of different materials, both natural and man-made or synthetic. Include an example of a metal, plastic, wood, rock, paper, rubber and cork. Add one or two less familiar materials, such as clay, pumice, natural sponge or sheep's wool.

Show the materials to the children, and question them about the various materials: what they are and where they come from or how they are made. Provide help and guidance regarding those materials that the children are less familiar with.

● Ask the children to think of as many ways as they can of sorting the materials. They may use categories of colour, shape, texture, transparency, whether the materials float or sink, what they are used for, whether or not they are attracted by a magnet, and whether they are natural or man-made. Encourage the children to develop a collection of adjectives to describe the materials.

● The children can record their findings with simple labelled sketches. Alternatively, they can prepare simple charts, each consisting of two columns headed with pairs of properties, such as 'Float' and 'Sink' or 'Attracted to a magnet' and 'Not attracted to a magnet'.

Electricity

Collect together examples (or pictures) of objects which rely on mains electricity and batteries and ask the children to group these examples or pictures. Discuss why sometimes electricity is used from batteries and sometimes from the mains. This provides an opportunity to reinforce safety issues. Explain that, while it is perfectly safe to experiment with torch batteries, they should never experiment with mains electricity.

Green plants as organisms

Safety: Be careful to ask about any allergies before letting children handle plants. Ensure they wash their hands thoroughly afterwards.

● Build up as large and as varied a collection of house plants as possible. Encourage the children to observe the plants closely and to be responsible for watering them.

● Let the children examine a common garden weed, such as a groundsel or shepherd's purse plant. Ask them to identify, then draw and label, the roots, stems, leaves, buds and flowers of their plant. They could examine one of the flowers with a hand lens. *Can you see the different parts of the flower? Can you grow some of the seeds from the plant?*

• Cut out pictures from plant and seed catalogues and stick them on to thin card. The pictures can then be used to help the children learn the names of common flowering plants, fruits and vegetables and to realise that many of the foods we eat come directly from living plants. They can also be used to help the children learn the names of the parts of a plant. You could write plant names on separate cards so that the children can match names and pictures.

Living things in the environment

The playground

Search the playground for plants, recording lichens, mosses, grasses, and so on. Note any animal life as well. Ask the children to try and describe the sorts of places where certain things are found. *Are there any differences between sunny and shady places and between damp places and dry places?* (If your playground is very barren, try to arrange a visit to a park or country centre to give your pupils the opportunity for this sort of exploration.)

Different environments

Make a collection of pictures of animals and plants which live in different environments. You may prefer to restrict the pictures to animals and plants which live in climatic extremes, for instance plants and animals of hot deserts and of the polar regions. Discuss how these living things are able to survive in their particular environment. Pose the question: *How do plants and animals survive in different places in this country?*

Developing key areas

Grouping materials

The word 'material' is often used to mean 'fabric'. However, the Concise Oxford Dictionary defines material as 'matter from which a thing is made.' By this broad definition, which is that implied in Sc3: *Materials and their properties*, everything in the universe, including all living organisms, is made up of 'material'.

Investigating paper

• Make a collection of as many different types of paper as possible. Use these to make a class display. Label each paper with its main use. Paper is made of fibres and tearing it reveals the different fibre patterns. Provide the children with magnifiers or hand lenses so that they can see these and draw them. Can they devise a way of finding out which types of paper are translucent (let light through) and which are opaque? *How will you make your experiment fair?*

• Investigate the strengths of different kinds of papers. Have two clean tin cans, one slightly larger than the other, (or use a clean yoghurt pot instead of the smaller tin). Fix a square of paper over the top of the large tin with a rubber band. Stand the smaller container on top. Put weights (or marbles) in the smaller container until the paper below breaks. Compare other kinds of paper. *Is the experiment fair? Which kind of paper do you think will be the strongest? Which kind of paper is the strongest?*

• The children can go on to compare the strengths of different kinds of tissues, using the same method. *Are two tissues twice as strong as one tissue?* Ask them to devise a fair test to find out which kind of tissue absorbs most water.

Magnetic materials

• Let the children find out which objects and materials are attracted to a magnet. They will soon discover that objects made of iron or steel, or which contain iron or steel, are attracted.

● Use a magnet, a wire paper-clip and some sheets of paper to find out through what thickness of paper the magnet can pull the paper-clip. *What thickness of other materials will the magnet pull or push through?* (Try water, wood, cardboard, glass and plastic, for example.)

Heat conductors

To carry out this demonstration experiment, fill a rubber hot-water bottle with hot (**not** boiling) water. Lay the hot-water bottle on your desk and ask a volunteer to quickly touch the outside of the bottle. *Is it hot?* Lay a thin piece of wood on top of the bottle. Leave it there for two or three minutes. Ask a volunteer to place a hand on top of the piece of wood. *Does it feel hot? Does it feel warm?* Next place a large tin lid on top of the bottle and leave it there for two or three minutes. *Is it hotter or colder than the wood was?* Try other materials, such as a plastic plate, a china plate, some cardboard and paper, pieces of cotton and woollen materials and a copper coin.

Explain that materials which do not feel cold to the touch and which let heat through slowly are called **heat insulators**. Materials which feel cold to the touch and which let heat through quickly are called **heat conductors**.

Ask the children, *Which of the materials you used are heat conductors?* (Metals). *Which are heat insulators?* (Non-metals). *Which type of material would you use to keep fish and chips warm? Which would you use for picnic mugs?*

Fabrics

● *Which are the **hard-wearing** fabrics?* Devise a method of comparing pieces of fabric of different kinds. (Ensure the children use pieces which are all the same size.) Rub each fabric the same number of times with a piece of brick or stone and then compare the amount of wear. *Which fabric would make the best pair of trousers?*

● *Which fabrics are waterproof?* Collect some pieces of different fabrics and discuss how to make the experiment fair. Stretch the pieces evenly over plastic pots which are all the same size. (Pots you can see through are the best.) Hold the pieces of fabric in place with rubber bands. Pour an equal amount of water on to each of the fabrics, using a pipette or a small measuring jug. *Watch carefully. What do you think is going to happen? Which materials let a lot of water through? Which materials let a little water through? Which materials let no water through? Which material would make the best raincoat?*

Electricity

Safety: Draw the children's attention to the dangers of mains electricity. Warn them that, while small batteries are safe, they must **never** tamper with wires, plugs or appliances connected to the mains supply.

Batteries and circuits

With the children, collect examples of things which require batteries – toys, torches, radios, calculators, timers, and so on. (They can cut out pictures from magazines to supplement the collection.) Sort the objects and pictures into those that use batteries to make light, make heat, make sound and to make things move. Record the results on a simple table or pictogram. (The children could use a computer program for this.)

● Let the children create simple circuits using a single torch bulb in a holder, a battery and wires. While, in theory, the children can do this by discovery or trial-and-error, it is usually necessary to give help and guidance, particularly with ensuring that the connections between the wires and the lamp holder and battery are tight.

● When the children have mastered the simple circuit, show them how to introduce a simple switch, made of a small block of wood, two drawing pins and a paper-clip or strip of metal foil. Explain that the switch acts like a gate or moveable bridge in the circuit, breaking the circuit when the switch is 'off' and completing it again when the switch is 'on'.

● Show the children what happens when extra bulbs are added to the circuit. (In the simplest arrangement of wires, the more bulbs that share a battery, the dimmer the light from each bulb will be.) Then add more batteries to the original circuit. In this case, the light from a single bulb will be much brighter and the bulb will burn out unless the circuit is quickly disconnected.

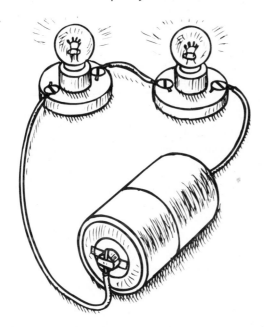

● Let the children make simple circuits using bells, buzzers or electric motors instead of light bulbs.

● Provide the children with different types of battery. Let them find the points (terminals) where the wires need to be connected to light a bulb.

● Follow this up by providing the children with pieces of wire which have not had the plastic insulation sleeve removed. *What effect does this have when we try to make a circuit to light a bulb?*

Electrical models

Encourage the children to design and make working models that incorporate a battery-powered light, such as houses made from cardboard boxes, model lighthouses made from plastic bottles, model theatres, or faces with illuminated noses.

Conductors and insulators

Let the children investigate which materials conduct (or carry) electricity and which do not.

Set up the circuit as shown in Figure 1. Ensure that all the connections are tight. If you now lay the blade of a screwdriver across the two drawing pins, the bulb should light. The blade of the screwdriver is a conductor (or 'carrier') of electricity. Now lay the handle of the screwdriver across the two drawing pins. Does the bulb light now? Materials which do not let electricity pass through them, so that the bulb does not light, are called insulators (non-metals such as glass, wood, rubber, plastics, and so on). Metal objects are conductors of electricity. (It may be easier to leave this apparatus more or less permanently set up and fixed onto a board which can be passed from desk to desk.)

Let the children record their results in a table consisting of two columns, one headed 'Conductors' and the other 'Insulators'.

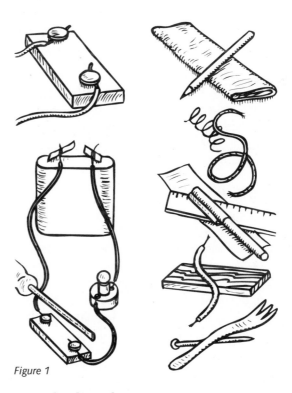

Figure 1

Steady-hand tester

Make a steady-hand tester. You will need a 30–50cm length of flexible, uninsulated wire. (Thin coat hanger wire is ideal.) Bend the piece of wire into a wavy line, making sure there are no sharp kinks in it. Bend another piece of the wire, about 30cm long, into a loop with a handle on it. Thread the wavy piece of wire through the loop. Support the wavy piece of wire in a wooden block with two narrow but deep holes drilled in it, or two big lumps of clay or Plasticine. Connect the tester

Science

to a bulb in a bulb holder with a battery. Wrap a short length of insulating tape (or sticky tape) around the wavy piece of wire where it enters the base. The bulb will not then light when the tester is at rest.

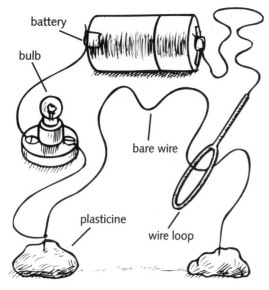

Let the children experiment with the steady-hand tester. Point out that it is really a type of switch since the circuit is completed when the wire loop touches the wavy piece of wire. If you can bear the noise, you can replace the bulb with a bell or buzzer!

Light without wires

How many ways can the children find of lighting a 1.5V (or a 1.25V) torch bulb without using electrical wires? Provide them with objects such as a coat-hanger, a metal can, scissors, paper-clips, coins, keys, or metal knives and forks. (They can, of course, look for other suitable objects in the classroom.) Tell them to make labelled drawings of all the circuits that work.

Light

● Blindfold one child as thoroughly as possible and ask another to lead him or her around the classroom. Discuss the problems of not being able to see because everything is dark. *What would it be like to be blind?*

● Investigate the use of lights and colours of signals, including traffic lights, railway signals, red flags, semaphore signals, road signs, hazard warning lights and the flashing lights used by the emergency services.

Shadows

● Work in the playground on a sunny day. Discuss what a shadow is and how it is made. *How can you make your shadow change its shape? Can you make a tall, short, wide or narrow shadow? Is it possible to lose your shadow? Can you make your shadow into a funny or frightening shape?* Organise the children into pairs and ask them to play 'shadow tag'.
Safety: This activity needs plenty of space since the children may well be running while looking at the ground and could easily collide with other children or objects.

● Use a clear bulb in a desk lamp or table lamp to cast shadows on a stretched piece of white sheet. Make a shadow play or pantomime.

● *Do shadows change during the day?* Let the children stand in the playground early on a bright morning and, working in pairs, draw around their partner's feet and shadow with chalk. Return later and get them to stand on their original foot marks. *Where is the shadow now? Is it still the same size? What has happened to make the shadow change?*

Sound

The physics of sound is difficult. The idea that sound is caused by a rapidly moving object which sends sound waves travelling through the air or through an object is rather an abstract one for children to grasp.

Safety: The ear drum is delicate. Children should be warned of the dangers of poking things in their ears and of the damage that can result from persistent exposure to loud sounds.

Using their ears

● Sounds are all around us, but being aware of sound is not necessarily the same thing as listening. There can be too much noise around for us to be able to distinguish individual sounds. Children often have to be taught to listen. Go on a listening walk around the school. Let the children listen to, and record in their notebooks or on a clipboard, both natural and man-made sounds. *Which types of sounds are most common around the school?*

● Some animals have very large ears for their size. Collect pictures of animals with large ears and discuss why the animals might need them. (The large ears of some animals, including elephants, act as a radiator to help cool their bodies, as well as being used for hearing.) *Would we be able to hear soft sounds better if we had large ears?* Let the children make 'ears' from thick paper or thin card and fix them over their own ears. Ask: *What do you think is going to happen? Can you hear better with the larger ears? How can you make the test of the larger ears fair?*

Visible vibrations

● Reinforce the idea of vibrations by making them visible. The simplest way is to lay a ruler on the edge of a table and, holding it firmly with one hand, twang the end projecting over the table with the other hand. A vibration will be seen to be a fast to-and-fro movement. Ask, *How can we alter the loudness of the sound made by a vibrating ruler?* (The harder we flick the ruler, the larger the vibrations, and the louder the sound.) *How can we make high and low notes with the ruler?* (Vary the amount of ruler projecting over the edge of the table.) The longer the ruler, the lower the note. (Depending on the maturity of your pupils you may need to discuss 'ruler twanging' as a generally acceptable idea!)

● Inflate a balloon. Let the air out slowly by stretching the neck. Notice how the mouth of the balloon vibrates as it makes sounds. Inflate the balloon again. Carefully attach its mouth to a whistle or flute. *Can you make the whistle or flute play a tune?* Discuss (or demonstrate) how bagpipes work.

● Encourage the children to feel their throats as they whisper a message, and again when they shout it. Ask them: *What do you notice?* (As the voice gets louder, the vibrations get bigger and

Science

easier to feel.) Explain that we make sounds by forcing air from our lungs through flexible but stretched vocal cords which cause vibration. (Allowing air to pass through the stretched neck of a balloon, as in the previous activity, is a good model for this.)

● To reinforce the connection between sound and vibrations, lay a sheet of tissue paper over the loudspeaker of a transistor radio. Carefully sprinkle sugar or salt on the paper. Turn on the radio and gradually turn up the volume. Observe how the grains of sugar or salt jump up and down in time to the vibrations.

Sounds without seeing

● Organise a quiz of mystery sounds. In this game children take it in turns to be out of sight behind a screen. The child behind the screen makes a sound which the rest of the class try to identify. Suitable sounds include snipping scissors, crackling a crisp packet, bouncing a ball, whirling marbles in a jar, shaking water in a bottle, and so on.

● Blindfold a child while another makes soft sounds a little way away from him or her. Ask the blindfolded child to point to where the sounds are coming from. Can the subject child locate the sounds as easily if one ear is covered?

Varying the pitch

● Use thread to tie a small bag to one end of a large rubber band. Fasten the other end of the rubber band to a piece of wood with a nail or drawing pin. Lay the whole apparatus on a table so that the bag hangs over the edge of the table. Lay two pencils a little way apart under the rubber band.

● Place a small weight or marble in the bag. Pluck the rubber band. Notice the pitch of the note produced. Add further weights to the bag. *How does the pitch of the note change?* Now see what effect varying the distance between the pencils has. (The more the rubber band is stretched, within reason, the higher the note that is produced.)

● Make a collection of different musical instruments (or pictures of musical instruments) and discuss how each of them works. *What has to be done to them to make sounds? How is the pitch of the sound varied? How is the volume of the sound varied?* Encourage the children to design and make some musical instruments of their own.

How does sound travel?

Vibrations and sounds will pass through air and other gases, water and other liquids and solids. The next few activities make use of these facts.

● Listen through an inflated balloon to the sounds made by a ticking clock or watch (the ticking sound travels through air). Now carefully fill the balloon with water, tie the bottom and place it between the ticking clock and your ear. *Does sound travel through water?*

● Will sounds pass through wood? Listen to a watch ticking. Lay it face up on one end of a wooden table, place the ear against the other end. Alternatively, place one end of a wooden dowel rod, at least a metre long, against a watch placed on the floor. Listen to the other end.

● Place children on either side of a wall. If one child places his or her ear against the wall, can he or she hear a tap, a whisper, or a ringing sound from the other side?

82   *Primary teacher* YEARBOOKS   TEACHING YEAR TWO

● Investigate string telephones. Use two plastic pots with a small hole in the bottom of each. Thread a long piece of thin string through the pots and attach the ends to matchsticks inside the pots. The string should be held taut. If one child whispers into one pot, another child will be able to hear what is being said when the second pot is held over the ear. (They should cover their free ear with their hand.) *What is the longest telephone you can get to work? If the string is not tight, can you still hear? What happens if we tie knots in the string? What happens if we tie two sets of telephones together in the middle of the string?* Encourage the children to plan and carry out their own investigations such as: *Which string makes the best telephone? What happens if wire is used? What happens if the size of the mouthpiece or earpiece is changed?*

● During a class PE session, ask the children to lie down in a large circle with you in the centre. Ask them to lower and lift one ear to and from the floor, covering their other ear, while you tap the floor very gently with a pencil. Ask them, *What do you notice?* Repeat the activity using a rubber mat between the ear and the floor. *What is happening to the sound?* (The sound is muffled because the mat has absorbed the sound.)

Different sounds

● Collect a set of tuning forks and experiment with them. Ask the children to observe the differences between the tuning forks. They may suggest length, thickness, weight and material. *How do these affect the sound the forks make? Can you make the sound from a tuning fork louder?* (Tap it harder.) *How can you show the tuning fork is vibrating?* (One method is to place the vibrating tuning fork in a bowl of water. A series of concentric waves may then be seen forming on the surface of the water.)

● Pour different quantities of water into five similar-sized glass bottles. (Wine bottles are best for this activity, although close adult supervision is necessary). Tap each bottle in turn with a metal spoon and listen to the notes produced. *Which bottle produces the highest sound? Which produces the lowest sound?* Ask the children to blow across the top of the bottles and listen to the notes produced. *Does the same thing happen?* Suggest they record their observations. *Why do you think there are different notes?* (Explain to the children that the bottle holding the least water, and therefore the most air, produces the lowest sound. The column of air in the bottles is vibrating.)

If the water in the bottles is coloured (with a little poster paint or food dye), the children can compose simple music and record it by using colour-coded notation symbols or pictures.

● Make simple pan-pipes by cutting plastic drinking straws to different lengths. Arrange the straws in length order, keeping them level across the top. Tape them securely together and then blow across the top to create a pan-pipe type of sound.

Sound volume

● Ask the children to listen to a whistle being blown (or a handbell being rung) at the far end of the playground. Then compare the volume when it is blown (or rung) close by. (Stress to the children that bells or whistles must never be rung directly into other people's ears.)

● Reinforce the concept of sound appearing fainter the more distant the source by playing the 'volume game'. Ask the children to stand in the middle of the room. Gradually, turn down the volume on a radio or cassette player. As you do this the children move towards you so that they can hear the music better. As you turn up the volume, they move away from you.

● *How close must a watch be for its ticking to be heard?* Test each ear separately to obtain average results. Do all the tests under fair (identical) conditions. Afterwards the children can plot bar-charts of some, or all, of the results.

Life processes

Humans and other animals

● Make a collection of pictures of people and other members of the animal kingdom, including birds and invertebrate animals ('minibeasts'). Spread the pictures out in front of a group of children and discuss the people and animals shown in the pictures. Ask such questions as: *What do all the people and animals have? What do some animals have which people do not? What do some people have which animals do not? Do all animals have legs?* Let the children sort the pictures into groups of 'Have' and 'Have not'. Examples of subjects used for groupings could be 'legs', 'feathers', 'hair' or 'fur', 'tails', 'wings', 'hands'.

The children can construct a table consisting of two columns showing the features humans and other animals have in common and the features that are different.

Animals in the classroom

● Keep a pet animal, such as a gerbil, in the classroom, even if for only a week or two. This will extend and supplement the work on the features of living things. With suitable hygienic precautions, the children can take it in turns to look after the animal. A list of tasks for the animal keepers to follow can be drawn up to ensure that the pet lives a healthy and safe life. After all the children have had responsibility for looking after the pet, they will be able to make comparisons, perhaps in the form of a table, of the things that animals do that are similar to humans, including how the pet moves, breathes, feeds, grows, produces waste materials, and uses its senses.

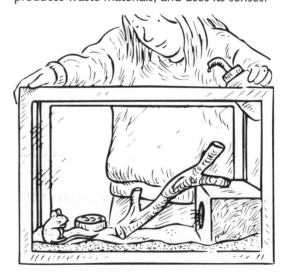

● Collect, or purchase, the eggs or caterpillars of butterflies and moths. Ensure that an abundant supply of the appropriate food plant is available. If you have collected eggs or caterpillars, this will be the same kind of plant the eggs or caterpillars were found on. Keep the eggs or caterpillars until the life cycle of the insect is completed (in warm weather this should take about two or three weeks). Encourage the children to keep a diary of their work. Do not let the children handle the caterpillars (some kinds have hairs that can produce an allergic reaction). Move the caterpillars gently, using a small paintbrush and plastic spoon.

(Insect Lore Europe, PO Box 1420, Milton Keynes, MK14 6LY Tel: 01908 200794 supplies a Butterfly Garden. This is a complete kit in which to raise butterflies.)

● Slugs and snails are common in cities and the country. Keep two or three in a large plastic sandwich box, an ice-cream container or an old aquarium. Put a layer of moist soil or compost in the bottom and cover this with a layer of damp, decaying tree leaves, pieces of bark, moss and one or two stones. Feed the slugs or snails on cabbage, lettuce, stinging nettles or dandelion leaves. Cover the container with muslin or with polythene or 'cling film' with small air-holes in it. Keep the container away from bright lights, heaters and radiators. Moisten the soil and dead leaves if they begin to dry out and put fresh food in the cage when the original begins to decay. *Which foods do slugs and snails prefer? How do they react to vibrations, sudden noises, torch light and other stimuli?*

● Put a pond snail in a jar of water together with a sprig of water weed. Let the children take it in turns to watch the snail for periods of, for example, half an hour. *How many times does the snail have to come up to the surface to breathe?* Compare water snails of different species and sizes. *Do they all breathe at the same rate?* Plot the results of this activity on a simple block graph so that comparisons can be made.

Green plants as organisms

Safety: Ask the children about any allergies they know they have before they handle any plants. Ensure they always wash their hands afterwards.

Plant spotting

Go on a plant-spotting tour of the school grounds. Look for cultivated and wild plants and for any unusual places where plants are growing, such as on walls and the trunks of trees and between paving slabs. Try to find some of the smaller green plants such as mosses, algae and ferns, as well as observing the larger ones such as trees. Explain that weeds are simply plants growing where they are not wanted. Encourage the children to use reference books to identify their 'finds' and to record their observations by drawing or painting the plants.

A tree survey

Carry out a tree survey in and around the school. *Which kind of tree is most common? Which tree is tallest? Which tree has the largest leaves? Which has the smallest leaves? Which of the trees are evergreen and which are not?* Allow the children to decide what other features to include in their survey. Use some of this information to make simple block graphs.

Growing things

● Make a collection of fruits and seeds. Include fruits which are bright and juicy as well as those, such as nuts, which are brown and dry. Discuss what we use fruits and seeds for.

● Fix four clean eggshells onto saucers, using clay or Plasticine. Paint a face on each eggshell and fill all of the eggshells with cotton wool. Leave the cotton wool in one eggshell dry, and moisten the cotton wool in the other three. Sprinkle cress seeds or grass seeds on the cotton wool in all four eggshells. Put the dry 'egg-person' on a sunny window sill, together with one of the egg people containing wet cotton wool. Place one of the others in a dark cupboard and the last one in a refrigerator. *Which of the egg-people grows 'hair'? Does the 'hair' look the same in each case?* (The 'hair' grown in the dark is not green because the plants need light to make chlorophyll. The seeds which are kept at low temperature and without water will not grow).

● Leave a potted plant, such as a geranium, in a place a little way from a window and water it. After a day or so, the children will be able to see how the plant has grown towards the light. If they turn the pot round, the plant soon grows

back towards the window again in its search for light. If the plant is fairly mature, it will bend towards the light each time it is turned round. It does this because the shoot responds positively to light which the plant needs in order to make food.

● Investigate plants and light further. Sow some cress or grass seeds in a pot of moist soil or compost. Make a small round hole at one end of a cardboard shoe box. Place the pot of seeds at the end of the box away from the hole and put the lid on the box. Stand the box on a sunny windowsill. After a few days the children can see that the seedlings are growing towards the light. *Will this experiment work with other seedlings? Can you make a runner bean seedling grow round in a circle?*

● Cover a potted plant with a clear, unperforated plastic bag and tie it around the main stem. Stand the plant in a sunny place. If the children look at the bag after three or four hours, they will see a film of water droplets inside. The water has been taken up from the soil and transported through the plant. It has evaporated from the leaves and stems and finally condensed on the inside of the bag.

● Not all plants reproduce solely with the aid of seeds. Some can be propagated artificially from other parts of the plant. Stand a freshly-picked willow twig or a sprig of garden mint, tradescantia or busy-lizzie, in a jar of water on a windowsill. Watch the plant stem grow underwater roots. Plant it in a suitable place outdoors and grow a new willow tree or plant.

Living things in the environment

Minibeasts

Prepare copies of a chart, like the one opposite, for each child or small group of children. Leave plenty of lines for animals in the 'Other' category, which cannot easily be identified. Suggest that the children search the school grounds for small animals. They can look on the walls of buildings, under bricks, stones and pieces of wood, on plants and in the soil. Use a trowel to dig in the soil. Each time a small animal is found, the children should tick the appropriate box in the chart to show where it was.

Use a plastic teaspoon and small paintbrush to pick the animals up. Put them in small transparent pots or dishes and look at each animal carefully with a hand lens. Ensure the children carefully put back any soil, bricks, stones or pieces of wood they move.

When the children have completed this part of the session ask them, *Where did you find most animals? Which kind of animals did you find most of?* If the children enter information from the charts on to a simple computer database (such as *Our Facts*, *Easy Works*, *Find IT*, *Datashow* or *Sparks*) they can use it to find out this kind of information.

Encourage the children to write a sentence or two to describe each kind of animal they found. (Less able children could prepare labelled drawings.) Let them describe the animal, for instance what colour it was, how many legs and explain why they think it was hiding where they found it.

Kind of animal	Where I found it						
	In the soil	On the soil	Under stones	Under wood	On a plant	In water	Somewhere else
Slug							
Snail							
Worm							
Woodlouse							
Centipede							
Millipede							
Spider							
Beetle							
Ant							
Earwig							
Butterfly							
Moth							
Other							

Make a wormery

Make a wormery to demonstrate the important role played by earthworms in the soil. Earthworms also recycle the materials in the leaves they drag into their burrows. Obtain a large clear plastic jar, damp soil, sand and small fallen tree leaves, a few live earthworms and a strip of black polythene or brown paper to cover the outside of the jar.

Put the damp soil and sand into the jar in clearly-defined alternate layers. If you wish, add a thin layer of powdered white chalk between one of the layers of soil and sand. Place the fallen tree leaves on top and add the live earthworms. Cover the outside of the jar with the black polythene or brown paper to exclude light and fasten it with rubber bands. Put a piece of stocking or muslin, held in place with a rubber band, over the top of the jar.

Keep the wormery in a cool place and make sure that the soil does not dry out. After about a week remove the covering to the jar. *What has happened to the soil and sand? Where are the leaves?* The children can see that the layers of soil and sand have been thoroughly mixed by the worms, while the leaves have been dragged down into the worms' burrows where they will rot, thus improving the soil fertility. The worm burrows also drain the soil and allow air into it where it can be breathed by plant roots. Return the worms to the garden when you have finished.

Bird feeders

Discuss with the children the birds that visit the school grounds. Make a bird-table and keep it well supplied with food (such as unsalted peanuts, fat, pieces of apple, table scraps, brown bread and water). Record the birds visiting the table over the course of a week. Choose three times of day to count the birds and plot their numbers on a graph. *When are there most birds?* Can the children devise an experiment to determine the food preferences of some common species of birds?

✿ Ideas bank

● Make a collection of items made from wood, plastic, paper, textiles, glass and metal. Ask the class to tell you what the materials are and what the items are used for, such as furniture, book coverings, footwear, containers. Let them make a note of the variety of uses of each of your chosen materials. Take the children on a walk around the school looking for all the different uses of wood, plastic, metal, paper, textiles and glass. Explain that you would like them to record their findings. Some children may wish to record with pictures, some with words. *Which material has the most uses? Which material has the fewest uses?*

● When using cylindrical batteries, you may find it is difficult to fix the wires to the battery terminals. Two simple ways of doing this are shown.

a) Fix the bare ends of the wires to paper-clips and hold these on to the terminals at each end of the battery with a rubber band or with sticky tape.

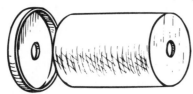

b) Punch a hole in the lid and base of a plastic film canister of the type used to contain 35 mm film.

Insert a brass paper fastener through the lid and base.

Push the wires through the paper fasteners.

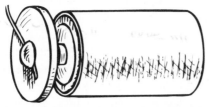

A 1.5V HP11 battery (also called R14 and 3014 size) should fit tightly inside the canister.

● Give each child (or small group) a 1.5V (or a 1.25V) torch bulb, a 1.5V battery and a narrow strip of aluminium kitchen foil. Ask them, *How many ways can you find to light the bulb?* Encourage them to record their findings on a table with two columns, headed 'Did light' and 'Did not light'. They can then record their successes and failures in the appropriate column and draw pictures of their ideas.

● Can the children devise a way of listening to soft sounds, such as the beat of their own heart or the ticking of a watch? One way is to make a simple stethoscope. This can be done by inserting a small funnel in each end of a short length of rubber or plastic tubing. One funnel is held to the ear while the other is held over the object making the soft sound. An alternative method is to make a large cone shape from paper or thin card held in place with sticky tape. If the pointed end is cut from the cone, it can then be used like an old-fashioned ear trumpet to channel soft sounds to one ear.

● With the help of the children, devise a sound or noise report form and then use it to conduct a sound survey of the different parts of the school. *Where are the loudest sounds heard? Do the sounds differ at different times of the day?* As a result of the discussion of the noise level (generally defined as 'loud or undesirable sound') the children may decide that there is a noise problem in their environment. Ask them to discuss what could be done about it. This discussion on noise could lead on to work on sound-proofing. (Sound is reflected off surfaces in a similar way to that in which light is reflected. When sound hits some surfaces it is reflected more than from others. When sound is not reflected well, it is being absorbed by the material.) Let the children investigate ways of 'silencing' an alarm clock.

● Plant fast-germinating seeds of alfalfa, mung beans, mustard or cress. Sprinkle them in pots of garden compost and keep them moist, or grow them on moist gravel, cotton wool or kitchen roll. They will germinate within a week. *Which type of seed grows first?* Draw the stages in growth of some of the seedlings.

Assessment

When you have finished the work with your Year 2 class, you will have a good idea as to whether the children enjoyed the topics and which style of teaching was most effective. You should also be able to judge how much the children have learned. Now is the time to evaluate each topic against the criteria with which you started.

What do they know?

There is no set list of facts they should know, but all the children should have gained something, even if that something varies from child to child. In Year 2 you might expect most six- to seven-year-olds to know:

- the basic life processes of humans, plants and animals, and the factors influencing them (Sc2);
- the names of the parts of a plant (Sc2);
- the basic requirements necessary when caring for plants and animals (Sc2);
- how to link living things to their particular environment (Sc2);
- how to make simple observations of habitats (Sc2);
- that there are lots of different materials (Sc3);
- how to examine and compare materials (Sc3);
- how to identify the most appropriate materials for a wide range of situations (Sc3);
- how to identify a wide range of sounds and be able to sort them in terms of loud and soft (Sc4);
- how we hear and what factors affect how loud we hear sounds (Sc4);
- how to recognise and name a wide variety of light sources (Sc4);
- that darkness is the absence of light (Sc4);
- that light cannot pass through some materials (Sc4);
- how shadows are formed (Sc4);
- that we see because light enters our eyes (Sc4);
- about things which need electricity to make them work (Sc4);
- why electricity is dangerous (Sc4);
- how to make a simple circuit which works a bulb, bell or buzzer (Sc4);
- what happens if a circuit is broken (Sc4);
- how to make a simple switch (Sc4);
- how to make the bulb in a circuit brighter or dimmer (Sc4).

Science

What can they do?

Most children should be able to:
- describe objects and materials (Sc1);
- describe things that happen (Sc1);
- identify a number of questions which can be investigated, in familiar situations (Sc1);
- recognise the need for a fair test (Sc1);
- explain what a prediction is and how it differs from a guess (Sc1);
- suggest what observations should be made and suitable ways of measuring these (Sc1);
- record their predictions and results (Sc1);
- present their findings using charts, pictograms and simple bar charts (Sc1);
- provide explanations that relate to scientific knowledge (Sc1);
- suggest improvements to investigations (Sc1).

What have they experienced?

The children should have:
- examined a variety of living things;
- handled a variety of materials;
- carried out simple experiments under guidance;
- devised their own simple experiments under guidance;
- investigated a variety of local habitats.

How have they made their knowledge public?

The children should have discussed their work with others and displayed their work through drawings, simple models, graphs and tables and, where possible, by means of short sentences written with your help.

History

At the end of Year 2, infant history will be completed, but traditional history, featuring significant past events and the lives of the famous, is just beginning. In Year 2, when history starts to emerge in its literary clothes, it also plays a role in furthering core curriculum aims in English, something that is especially significant in this year of the SATs.

There is plenty of scope for teachers to choose their own history topics. The National Curriculum suggests that:

History fires pupils' curiosity about the past in Britain and the wider world. Pupils consider how the past influences the present, what past societies were like, how these societies organised their politics, and what beliefs and cultures influenced people's actions. They see the diversity of human experience, and understand more about themselves as individuals and members of society. What they learn can influence their decisions about personal choices, attitudes and values.

Children will be given opportunities to consider how the past influences the present, what people and societies in the past were like. They begin to develop a chronological framework for their knowledge of significant events and people; see the diversity of human experience, and understand more about themselves.

Their activities should involve finding and assessing evidence and reaching conclusions through research and arguing their viewpoints.

As this content covers Year 1 as well as Year 2, the first priority is to sort out which parts you are to teach. The school policy should, in fact, specify this but, whatever the policy says, it is as well to check what the children have actually covered in Year 1. You want to avoid unnecessary repetition.

As there is scope for choice, it is not possible to be definitive about what history you will teach, but it is likely that teaching about past events, especially notable anniversaries and commemorations (such as the Coronation, the Battle of Britain, Gunpowder Plot), might occur at any time during the infant stage, including Year 2. Most schools prefer to leave a specific history project and famous people until Year 2.

Some, if not all, of your history will be done within general topics, but teachers usually find time in Year 2 for one specific project with a mainly historical focus. But which project? Which period?

Many schools choose 'The Victorians'. Alternatively, given the proximity of the millennium, the project 'The turn of the century' may be appropriate and would provide the opportunity for topical connections, for instance you could talk about the 1900 exhibitions and the Millennium Dome.

It has been shown that children of this age cope more easily with large chunks of time rather than small divisions, so you might find it interesting to take a large leap back in time and study a period such as the Stone Age which, incidentally, is unlikely to be tackled in any other key stage. (Avoid studying 'Dinosaurs' because there is no human link.)

You will probably want to explore festivals and anniversaries, so it is worth looking at less obvious festivals such as the school's 50th anniversary; St George's Day; Trafalgar Day; Remembrance Day; The Battle of Britain Day; perhaps, even, Thanksgiving.

Do not choose your 'famous people' studies arbitrarily, look for local or topical links. For example, after a maritime disaster one school studied Grace Darling; after a visit from a Red Cross representative, one class looked at the lives of famous doctors and nurses. Statues in the local park can provide excellent starting points for this sort of work. Everywhere has someone famous connected with it – even if it is a tenuous connection. Research your local environment for ideas.

However you choose to study history in this year, make sure that the children can still link it with the world they know. Things they see on television and video can provide accessible starting points. Keep infant history simple and direct as well as highly visual and tactile – meet the retired teacher, make rubbings of the coal-hole cover, dress up in the Fifties clothes, and so on.

What should they be able to do?

Children of this age may take a keen interest in the past. They have begun to grow in their awareness of time, in their use of time vocabulary and in their capacity to remember. If children are given appropriate tasks, it is surprising just how much history many of them can cope with. However, Year 2 children should not spend as much school time on history as older children and therefore aims and expectations must still be kept few and reasonable. Historical skills and knowledge are acquired slowly so do not worry if you repeat or reinforce aspects of historical learning that the children covered earlier in the school.

Below is a guide to suitable expectations for the majority of six- to seven-year-olds in relation to the subject's key elements.

The five key areas include the skills and ideas essential to the subject. You do not need to teach each key area every time you teach history but they will be covered gradually over the key stage.

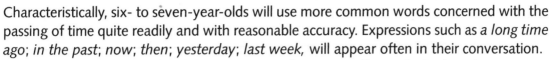

Key area: Chronological understanding

Characteristically, six- to seven-year-olds will use more common words concerned with the passing of time quite readily and with reasonable accuracy. Expressions such as *a long time ago*; *in the past*; *now*; *then*; *yesterday*; *last week*, will appear often in their conversation.

Clearly the young child's ability to cope with time is still very limited – when you are struggling with two and three digit numbers, dealing with tens of thousands is problematic. But some children do begin to appreciate dates as a kind of 'word label' and may know what year it is now or the year they were born in. You may start, selectively, to use dates in this way. Even so, remember that not all children will be able to cope even with a simple notion such as 'last week'. The great majority of six- and seven-year-olds will, however, be able to distinguish past time from present time, know that the past existed and that it was different from the present.

More able children can exhibit a surprising sophistication when dealing with time, largely because they have a more highly-developed linguistic ability. They may tell 'clock' time with considerable skill and even have an understanding that the past can be divided up into periods of time and may occasionally use terms such as 'Victorians', 'Tudors' or 'Turn of the century' correctly.

Year 2 children have moved on in their ability to place in time order a small number of objects of different ages. Many children will now not only cope with three objects quite readily (oldest – newest – one in the middle) but, where their knowledge allows, will deal with events in broadly the same fashion. Dates, other than in the case of exceptional children, will not be the method of ordering by time.

Key area: Knowledge and understanding of events, people and changes in the past

For the first time you can expect children to know some history within the traditional understanding of the phrase. By the end of Year 2, they should know, and be able to recall, some facts about the past. For example, 'Queen Victoria ruled Britain 100 years ago.' They will know of some famous people, such as Guy Fawkes, and be able to recount some specific events, but they will also be able to make general distinctions between their own time and the past. ('There were no cars in those days.')

Adult history deals with causes and consequences and the positing of hypotheses about why events happened and why people acted as they did. Infant children are not mature enough to cope with these kind of intellectual devices but they can start to recognise that people in the past had reasons for their actions. Of course, this is at a simple level of understanding. Children first become aware of the past as a vague amorphous mass, so early understandings tend to arise in simplistic forms, thus their past will be full of sharp demarcations such as between 'goodies' and 'baddies' and their appreciations of why people acted the way they did will be of the same order. You can expect that brighter children will ask and begin to seek answers to questions about the past.

Key area: Historical interpretation

The past is presented to us and interpreted in many different ways; in museums, books, television programmes, and so on. At the end of Year 2, children should not only be able to distinguish between past and present, but also to identify some of these ways in which the

past is represented. Their vocabulary will be expanding to help them to make these distinctions. For example, they will know what a museum is.

Year 2 children take great delight in recognising different versions or interpretations of familiar stories, 'The Princess and the Peanut' for instance, and there are many of these types of story with which to amuse and challenge them. Developing children's habits of perception helps to prepare the ground for later work on historical interpretations: *How is this 'interpretation' different from what we know?*

Key area: Historical enquiry

This key area focuses on how we find out about the past, it is about evaluating evidence and sources. Even though Year 2 children will not hypothesise in the same way as adult historians they can observe and ask questions.

Most children should have developed enough skill in observation to enable them to answer simple questions from their observations. Given a source of information, such as a portrait or artefact, they can observe, question and answer. All three of these activities will, of course, be at a fairly simple level of understanding. For example, faced with a photograph of the ageing Queen Victoria, they might ask 'What was she like?' Observations such as *old*, *important*, *unfriendly*, and so on might follow from examination of the picture. Some children might go beyond this, offering reasons for answers or questioning the conclusions of others, saying, for example, 'She is not really unfriendly she is just sitting still while her photograph is taken.'

Given appropriate practice and experience, Year 2 children will begin to cope with a range of historical sources. As much experience as possible in handling and discussing historical artefacts is desirable. Standing in a castle once used by a medieval knight, or holding a jug used by an ancient Roman, is as close as anyone can get to first-hand experience. Children's ability to engage in historical enquiry at Year 2 largely depends on the quantity and quality of their experience in handling evidence.

Documentary sources invariably pose problems for primary children, particularly infants, but a Year 2 child may still appreciate the function of say, a ration book or an old map. Pictures, however, are much more accessible, and children will appreciate that we can get some idea of what it was like in the past through old photographs and paintings.

Key area: Organisation and communication

The most skilful top infants can write coherently and at surprising length, and the majority of children will have begun to communicate adequately in written form. Because the most able often catch the writing bug at this age, the gap between them and the least able can be quite wide. In communicating awareness and understanding of the past, talk will still predominate, although all children should be using pictures and writing to some extent.

The language skills that are critical to children becoming successful learners are also essential to their successful communication of historical understanding (as well as success in end of Key Stage 2 English SATs). Through their studies of the past, Year 2 children can practise listening, remembering and responding (speaking and listening) – especially perhaps through historical stories; they can read information and stories as well as use reference books to find out information (reading); and plan, draft, revise and present their work in written form (writing).

Planning for history

Record the history you will be teaching on your long-term planning sheet. It does not matter what form your planning takes as long as it happens and it is written down. The best time for any specific history project is probably the early Spring term but you will make your own judgement on this. It may, perhaps, depend on the anniversaries and people you choose to study and how you wish to place this topic in relation to significant features of the school year such as Christmas and SATs.

Secondly, make sure that you have collected together, or arranged to have access to, all the resources that you will need. As you are likely to be studying a particular historical period this year, you may want to order special book and artefact packages from your library and museum services. Remember yours may not be the only class studying the period you have chosen so make arrangements early. This will apply also to orders for radio and television broadcast notes. Story and picture books to read to the children and to place in the book corner need to be collected together, as do suitable pictures. Be aware that there are now many excellent commercially-produced collections for schools.

Thirdly, make classroom preparations for history. Fortunately there is very little to do other than to arrange for selective displays of relevant objects for the tinkering table. Timelines should be a feature of your classroom during specific projects. (A general dated line for permanent reference is something for the junior stage.)

Allocating time

You may never teach a precisely measured quantity of history at this stage in the primary school, but you should have a target range of time in mind within which your teaching should fall. When you are doing your long-term planning will probably be the only time you will refer to it. A target time of 36 hours in a school year is reasonable at Key Stage 1 (approximately 3% to 4% of curriculum time) although, depending on the kind of topics that you choose, you might do considerably more. If in a particular term you are undertaking a major history topic, such as 'Stone Age Man' for example, then you might allocate 24 hours in that term and 12 hours in another term. It is not practical to try to allocate the hours week by week. This time target is a planning and reporting aid. Auditing with accountancy precision is not required.

Practical ideas

Key areas

Whatever activity you engage in, always ask yourself, *What are the children going to do?* Think always in terms of activity. The activity must be historically valid, not just busy work, and you can decide this with reference to the key areas. Does the activity further learning within the key areas? If not, examine your activity carefully.

Whatever topic you decide to do, it is important to observe a few basic rules:

● Do not make the project too complex.
● Keep it highly visual and active.
● Tell stories that grab the imagination.
● Never digress far from the evidence.

Making a start

Generating questions

Use games and classroom discussions to get the children generating questions which they might use in 'finding out' activities. For example, pass round a picture or object. Each child has to ask one question about it. Sort and organise the questions with the children's help. Where appropriate resources are available, ask the children to find the answers.

Developing key areas

Timelines

● Make a famous people timeline, preferably one that can be added to throughout the year.

This can be made using a clothes line on which you peg pictures of the people you study or historical figures mentioned during the year. Order is the key feature not dates. Using pegs allows the figures to be moved to accommodate events or additional people. You can also ask the children to practise arranging and rearranging events correctly. Year 2s can cope with the idea of fixed time markers – the year 1; the millennium; the second millennium. Use pictures to represent those dates (Birth of Christ/Battle of Hastings/ the Millennium Dome).

● Make an object or picture timeline within the project period to be studied. For example, if you are studying the Victorians you might have pictorial markers for Jubilee years; the Great Exhibition; the maiden voyage of SS Great Britain; the opening of Paddington station, and so on.

There are many variations on the timeline themes – time wheels; time ladders; time trains, and so on. A visual reference is very helpful for children when they are attempting to sort out the past but do keep it simple. World history timelines or whole-school timelines should be saved for later and clock face timelines are too sophisticated for this age-group.

Sequencing and sorting

● Sequencing objects or pictures is a time-related activity that can be developed a little at this stage. Try, for example, sequencing within the period chosen according to different criteria, for instance, clothes, transport. (Select and try different word combinations – *first, last, long ago, now, then, before, after, beginning, middle, end, most recent, most ancient, modern, old-fashioned.*)

● Sorting activities (individually with duplicated pictures or on the tinkering table with objects or pictures) can be fun. Choose a theme, for example childhood, toys or old people, and ask children to sort a selection of pictures into 'then' and 'now'. Objects or pictures can be put in a bag from which they can be drawn one at a time to be placed on the correct table (one table labelled 'Then', the other 'Now').

Words and names

● Make a 'words from the past' board. Ask children to pin up words they learn that are new or have a particular connection with the period. You may like to include modern words for comparison – swaddling bands/nappy. You could also include the names of famous people whose names arise during the course of study.

● An interesting variation, if you have the data, is to compare first names nowadays with the period you are studying. The Victorian period is often easy to do, especially if you teach in an old school and the original admission registers are still available (Albert versus Neil; Victoria versus Nathalie). Alternatively, children can ask elderly people what names were common in their classes at school. If your names from today include a range of ethnic names, Daljit, Parvati, Siu Yin and so on, you will have a wide new area for discussion. Be prepared for it with some basic knowledge about the history of immigration. The children could print the names out using DTP and select period-style typefaces.

Pictures and stories

● Create two giant collages ('now' and 'then') on which children can pin or stick pictures on a chosen theme, for example transport; food and cooking; farming; schooldays.

● Find or draw pictures that illustrate a historical story that you have told to the class. (Old books are a good source but you will need to be able to photocopy them or cut the pictures out. If you can't draw, you may be able to persuade an artistic parent, friend or colleague to draw them for you.) Choose five or six pictures showing key events of the story. Devise games and activities using the illustrations to encourage the children to explore the events and the sequence in which they happened. For example, they can be sorted chronologically according to whether they illustrate the beginning, middle, or end. Children can then be asked to choose the three most important pictures. Display them all on a line (use velcro fixing or pegs) and remove two or three key pictures. Can the children remember the missing links?

● Place the story pieces on a target, using velcro again, with the most important picture near the centre and the least important at the edge. What are the reasons for the choices made?

Choose the story you use for this type of work carefully – you do not want to interrogate a good story to death.

Frames for writing and thinking

● Use various sentence starters to encourage children to develop written answers and to think clearly. For example:
I think that...
I know this because...
The reason is...
Devise similar questions appropriate to the tasks.

Use 'prompt' sheets to help children carry out investigations or interrogate evidence. For example:
I can see that...
I can work out that...
I need to find out...

● Another frame for thinking is the *True/False/ We have no evidence* game. There are various ways of playing this. One way is to draw three sets, one for each heading, and then provide on cards a series of statements about a picture or an object. The children discuss each statement and decide into which set it should be placed. (Some children could do this activity on the computer.)

Groups of children can make up their own statements on card to be passed on to a different group to sort.

Detective game

One way to develop children's understanding that we learn about people in the past by exploring evidence is to use the 'waste-paper bin' detective game. Empty a class waste bin (ideally one from a different class) on to newspaper and ask, *What can you tell about the people in that class from what's in the bin?* (What do the orange peel and the pencil shavings tell us has been going on?) This is a good activity to use before a museum visit.

Revision game

At the end of a history topic, one way to test what the children have retained is to write the name of a period object or perhaps even an event on to a piece of card and put it where it cannot be seen. The children then ask you questions in order to try to find out what it is. You are only allowed to answer 'yes' or 'no'. Children can, of course, also take the hot seat.

Visits

Visits start to become a more worthwhile option with top infants so if there is a site within reasonable distance that fits your project then use it. Is there a medieval castle? A Victorian house? A suitable museum?

Ideas bank

● Use tape recorders with the children who are less able, not only to record answers but to record the children's questions as well. The latter exercise can be particularly useful when children are preparing to interview an adult about the past.

● Observational drawing is a good way to focus children on historical artefacts. They can make a catalogue of 'Objects we have studied'.

● Children can create museum display cards for objects and pictures used during your project.

Early man

A few more adventurous cross-curricular suggestions for a Year 2 project on Early Man are given below to show what is possible. (These have all been done in schools.)

◗ Make your own cave (in the classroom or in the school grounds) and re-enact primitive living patterns.

◗ Re-create cave paintings using natural materials for both brushes and paint.

◗ Construct coil pots and simple pottery utensils. (One junior school fired their pots in a home-made sawdust kiln in the playground!)

◗ Give children experience of weaving, spinning or dyeing using natural materials.

◗ Create and enact a burial ritual in a long barrow based on what is known. Make up music to accompany the ceremony using primitive instruments.

◗ Get children to tell stories of hunting adventures to the tribe (the rest of the class!). Try to carry out these sort of re-enactments in a suitably atmospheric place – a clearing in a wood, a darkened classroom by the light of a candle or a torch-and-red-paper 'fire' or even in a genuine historic site if you are near a suitable one. (A class once had a splendid end to an early history project telling each other stories gathered round the Uffington White Horse high on the windswept Berkshire Downs.)

◗ Grind corn on a stone quern.

◗ Try cultivating a strip of land using only primitive tools.

◗ Let the children see a demonstration of flint knapping.

◗ Bury some artefacts and simulate an archaeological dig (set up a grid over a small area of land and 'map' the finds). Choose your artefacts carefully to give clues to the lives of the primitive people who left them.

The children will remember activities like these when they have forgotten all their other history.

Assessment

Because history has begun to mean something to six- and seven-year-olds, it is possible to make judgements about their performance in the subject. The National Curriculum makes it clear that 'in deciding on a pupil's level of attainment (in history) at the end of the key stage, teachers should judge which description best fits the pupil's performance'.

All that is required is that you make an overall assessment, so the level descriptions must be taken *as a whole* and not dismembered to make separate targets or tick lists. Year 2 children generally fall within the range Level 1 to Level 3, although some may still be working towards Level 1. (Refer to the National Curriculum for the level descriptions.) You will find it helpful to refer to the performance indicators ('What should they be able to do?' see pages 92–95) when you come to make a final judgement at the end of the year as to *best fit*.

Geography

During Key Stage 1, children learn about places and small localities, starting with their local area. This will be the immediate vicinity of the school, including the school buildings, the grounds and surrounding area within easy access, probably within walking distance for the children. They can compare this with contrasting localities of a similar size. For example, they can learn about another part of the city in which they live, a locality in a nearby village, in a neighbouring town, or in 'natural' countryside. Alternatively, you may prefer to choose an overseas locality with which you yourself are familiar.

Whichever your school has chosen, there are four key areas of geography in which your pupils should be progressing. These are:

- geographical enquiry and skills;
- knowledge and understanding of places;
- knowledge and understanding of patterns and processes;
- knowledge and understanding of environmental change and sustainable development.

In Year 2 you will continue to develop these four key areas. The emphasis will still be on providing spatial experiences in school and in its immediate environment, extending children's language both for describing their environment and for talking about their experiences. You will also be working to improve and extend children's graphicacy skills by using pictures, diagrams, signs and symbols, maps and globes.

In their immediate natural and/or manufactured (man-made) environment the children should:

- explore and way-find through first-hand experience;
- have experiences using all their senses to develop wonder, curiosity, respect for people, cultures and places;
- share responsibility for its quality, becoming aware that their actions, and those of others, can improve or spoil it;
- develop a sense of self and their place in the home-setting and community, by talking about themselves, family, friends and events.

Introducing a range of localities

The children should also explore similarities and differences between their own immediate natural and/or manufactured environment and others with contrasting physical and/or human features. Aim to broaden their experience by introducing a range of localities, possibly in less depth: hot and cold (eg tropical and polar), wet and dry (eg rainforest and desert), near and far, north and south, natural and manufactured (built). Choose places with which you are familiar, with which the children in your class have connections or which are currently receiving coverage in the news.

You will, as a staff, decide whether or not to look at localities beyond the UK. It is difficult, educationally, to deny infant children opportunities to learn about distant localities but it is important to consider the cultural context. At an age when children are learning to

interpret their own 'Western' environment from their own (mostly) 'Western' cultural perspective, will they be confused by non-Western localities? Will bringing an emerging, conscious Western viewpoint to, say, an African locality, inculcate or reinforce stereotyping? Is it better to wait until Key Stage 2 to teach about developing countries, when children are a little more secure with their own culture, and better able to empathise? Perhaps an alternative is to choose distant but essentially 'Western' localities (Australasia, Canada, USA, Europe) to bring a global dimension into Key Stage 1 work. Of course, if you have a significant number of, for example, Afro-Caribbean or Asian children in your class, all contributing different cultural backgrounds and perspectives, then a different argument applies. But this philosophical discussion is one for your own staffroom.

What should they be able to do?

In Year 2, children should make progress in the four key areas of geography which will be integrated in the activities you provide, either in designated geography lessons or in topic or thematic work in which the geography is explicitly identified.

Key area: Geographical enquiry and skills

Children should develop and extend their ability to:
● understand and use geographical vocabulary, including following directions;
● respond to questions about places and environmental topics on the basis of information you provide, and begin to ask and seek answers to their own geographical questions;
● make, record, question, communicate and compare their own observations about places and environments from first-hand experience, practical activities and secondary sources such as photographs, videos and CD-ROMs;
● collect, record and represent information or measurements pictorially and graphically, and begin to analyse or explain it;
● carry out simple enquiries by undertaking fieldwork tasks and activities using and/or making maps, diagrams, photographs and other resources you provide.

Key area: Places

Most children should be able to recognise, describe, express views about and record:
● the main physical (landscape, weather and so on) and human (buildings, routeways, etc) features of their local area, and any other localities they study, using appropriate geographical vocabulary;
● that places change (due to seasonal effects, new buildings, and so on);
● that buildings and land are used for a variety of purposes (industry, housing, agriculture);
● the significance of location, why features are where they are, why things happen where they do; (for example, the location of the local shopping centre; where the buses stop);
● similarities and differences between the places they visit and study.

Key area: Patterns and processes

Children should respond to questions about:
● where things are (for instance, where their school is in relation to their homes);
● physical (natural) and human processes: why things are like they are (what happens to rainfall – water flows downhill and can move things);
● the pattern of how things change (for example, the pattern of the school day, how the weather changes through the day/year; the school year, a farming year; types of housing in older and newer areas nearby).

Key area: Environmental change and sustainable development

Most children should be able to:
● express their own views about physical and/or human features of their environment, recognising attractive and unattractive aspects (the aesthetics of the built environment);
● recognise that their environment changes and that people affect it (noise and air pollution from traffic; changes in the use of land);
● appreciate that the quality of the environment can be improved (by keeping the classroom quiet and tidy; by pedestrianising shopping centres).

These aspects are looked at in more detail in Practical ideas, although the focus is on geographical skills and enquiry – the tools of geography.

Practical ideas

 ## Developing key areas

Geographical vocabulary

Continue practising, and extending, the geographical language developed in the earlier years, including the language of direction, location, scale and distance, quality and aesthetics as well as the names of physical and human features of the natural and built environment. Children should be learning classifications (for instance, that houses, shops, streets, church, and so on all create a neighbourhood or village) and hierarchies (village, town, city).

I-Spy

Play geographical I-Spy, using walks, visits or pictures to introduce and practise the names of features and characteristics of the natural or physical environment, including landscape and weather, and the built or human environment, including settlements, economic activities, jobs, journeys and transport, water and vegetation in the environment. This is essential language preparation for Key Stage 2 themes.

Role-play

Encourage the children to act out scenes to do with shopping, industry, agriculture, transport and holidays at home and abroad.

Use photographs

Collect photographs of the local area and your chosen contrasting locality, taken in various weathers in all seasons at different times of the day. These can then be used by the children for recognition, matching, sorting, sequencing and talking activities. (Remember that it is very useful, and considerably cheaper, to have multiple sets of prints made at the time of processing.)

Word lists

Make geographical vocabulary lists including the features which give places their particular character. Some words, like weather vocabulary, will be universal but some will be specific to your school, your local area and your chosen contrasting locality.

Practise the vocabulary

Reinforce geographical language development using flash-cards, word banks and charts and playing games with them. Devote a regular part of the literacy hour to geographical words and stories. (While this is not strictly geography, it does practise and reinforce the vocabulary.)

Continued development

Development of geographical vocabulary and general knowledge is a continuous process, so many of the themes and ideas introduced in earlier years are, of course, still appropriate for Year 2. Children of this age are usually fascinated by specialist terminology, so do not be afraid to introduce new, long or complicated words.

Geographical knowledge

Continue to develop the children's geographical general knowledge.

● Create opportunities to talk about places the children have visited or where their relatives live. Alternatively, discuss places that have been mentioned in the news, or that the children have seen on television or encountered in stories.

● Extend their knowledge of local, national and global places and features, reinforcing the knowledge with pictures wherever possible. Locate the places and features on maps in atlases and on globes. Remember full conceptual understanding comes later. Use a computer package to create a data bank of geographical general knowledge.

● Each week give the children some new geographical facts – such as names of high mountains, long rivers, 'nestings' (for instance, *Nairobi is the capital city of Kenya, a country in the continent of Africa*, or *In Africa there's a country called Kenya with a capital city called Nairobi*). You could develop or adapt this into your own version of a geographical general knowledge quiz game.

● Play alphabet geography – put up an alphabet list each week and choose a theme, such as cities, countries or rivers. Invite the children to find the name of a city, country or river beginning with each letter of the alphabet. This can become quite a competitive activity – parents can also join in if they wish.

Geographical enquiry

At this stage, you will increasingly be encouraging the children to ask and seek answers to their own geographical questions. You will be extending their geographical thinking beyond 'observe and describe'. For example,

When studying places:
What is it? What is it like?
(observation, description)
What sort of place is it?
(categorisation, classification)
Is it like any other places you know?
(comparison, similarity and difference)
Where is it?
(location, distance, direction)
How can/did/will we get there?
(communications, time, cost)
Why is it like it is?
(conjecture, hypothesis, speculation)
Is this place changing? How?
(continuity and change, dynamics, time, spatial process, development)
Why do you think it is changing?
(cause and consequence, power (economic, social, political) in the sense of *Who or what has the power to sanction or cause change?*)
If it is a place the children have visited:
What do you feel about it? Do you like it?
(opinion, values, attitude)
What would it be like to live/work here?
(empathy)
If there is a problem, issue or something about the place the children do not like:
Why is it a problem/issue?
(opinion, explanation)
Is there anything you can do about it?
(action)

Place study

The questions above should help to form the framework for a place study, perhaps a study of the immediate locality of the school. They are challenging questions but Year 2 children are not too young to meet them. You will be preparing them to handle controversial geographical issues and introducing them to the idea that to some questions there is no one correct answer – there is a range of responses, because people have different opinions, some 'better' than others. (Later in their school careers, they will learn about consensus and decision-making.)

If, as a school, you have chosen to 'revisit' the local area each year, it is likely you will have selected a focus for each study (homes, shops and jobs, transport and journeys, and so on). These will give depth, and enable you to reinforce geographical skills and enquiry in a variety of different contexts.

Contrasting locality study

If you have chosen a nearby contrasting locality (such as a local industrial or agricultural area to contrast with the school's residential area) then you are likely to be able to include a visit in your study. However, if you have chosen somewhere further afield (a locality in the countryside or in another town, county or country) then you will be relying on video, maps, perhaps a photo-pack, and possibly personal experience and your own photographs.

Enquiry framework

● Whichever contrasting locality you choose, you should still use an enquiry or investigative framework based on geographical questions like those suggested on page 105. You will be encouraging children to **observe** and **describe**, and **compare** with their own locality in order to identify and explain similarities and differences. You may find it helpful to focus on the way of life of a family, finding out and explaining how they live in their place at this time (the effect of location on weather, on the food they eat, the clothes they wear, the housing they live in, the jobs they do).

● When focusing on photographs within your enquiry, ask different types of questions of the photographs. For example, if you are looking at a photograph of a shopping centre, you can use questions which are: **concrete** (*What can you see?*), **descriptive** (*What are the people doing?*), **speculative** (*What would they do if it started to rain?*), **reasoning** (*Why aren't the people wearing jumpers?*), **evaluative** (*Is this a good place to shop?*), **problem solving** (*How, or where, else could all these people do their shopping?*). These six types of question should be asked throughout the primary school – progression will be achieved through the challenge or complexity of the question and its context. (For some more ways to use photographs see page 107 'Interrogate pictures'.)

Graphicacy skills

Graphicacy, 'the essentially pictorial communication of spatial information', should be ranked alongside literacy, oracy and numeracy. To be graphicate is an important life skill.

● Children should continue to develop and use their graphicacy skills for:

▶ acquiring spatial information from pictures, photographs, diagrams, aerial photographs, maps, plans, globes and atlases, and in way-finding.

▶ giving or communicating spatial information, using pictures and diagrams, making maps and plans.

● To develop spatial or environmental awareness, the ability to make mental maps of their local area and further afield, and eventually to draw maps, children need to bring together experience, observation, perception, description (language), memory and recall, visualisation, sequencing and representation (drawing). Use practical classroom activities and opportunities to go for short walks around school, the school grounds, the neighbourhood and further afield so that the children can gain experience in developing these skills.

Way-finding

Take walks around the school, school grounds, and the local area or neighbourhood, and discuss them afterwards in the classroom.

Where am I?

Name a starting point familiar to the children. Describe a walk from this point using locational and directional language. Mention various landmarks en route. Encourage children to visualise the walk, then stop and ask *Where am I?* For example, a walk might start at the school gate and finish in the school library, having taken a circuitous route.

Interrogate pictures

Use pictures and photographs of the school, the school grounds, the locality of the school and a contrasting locality. (You may also like to include home-made videos.) In addition to using the six types of questions listed on page 106, encourage children to:

▶ give the picture a title (this requires them to look at the picture as a whole);

▶ identify features, and match name-labels of features to the picture;

▶ match a line drawing ('field sketch') to a photograph (for instance, give them three similar photographs and three line drawings and ask them to match them);

▶ construct a panorama from three or four overlapping photographs;

▶ make their own 'field sketch' from a photograph (initially by tracing, but eventually free-hand);

▶ articulate questions about the picture *If you met this person what would you ask her?*;

▶ suggest what happened just before or just after the photograph was taken.

Use diagrams

Encourage the children to make models and constructions from diagrams – especially 2-D representations of 3-D structures.

Different perspectives

● Take photographs of the school and its locality from unusual perspectives. Ask the children to match them to photographs of the same features taken from ground level. Discuss where the features are in relation to your classroom (distance, direction, route) and where the unusual views are taken from.

● Take three photographs (side, oblique and vertical view) of different children and locations; sort them into sets – for example 'same perspective', 'same child', 'same place'.

● Identify and label features on an aerial photograph of the school, and match it with a plan or map.

Use maps, plans, globes, atlases

● Use PVC floor maps (these can be written on with washable felt-tipped pens) to locate topical and familiar places.

● Use inflatable globes and ask the children to recognise land and sea. Introduce names of continents and oceans; compare with a rigid, mounted globe, orientating similarly.

● Identify and name specific features on a physical globe (mountains, rivers, plains). Identify countries and capital cities on a political globe.

● Have a range of picture and other atlases available in the book corner.

● Locate local journeys on a street map and longer journeys in a road atlas.

Reading and drawing maps

Just as children need to see texts, be read to and learn to read alongside before they can write stories, so they need to see maps, have maps 'read' to them, learn to read maps themselves and understand what a map is and its purpose, before they can draw their own. It is important that children are given opportunities to use real maps of all types.

Making pictures and diagrams, maps and plans

Throughout their school life children are often asked to draw maps of their journey to school. Try to draw such a map yourself – it is very difficult and requires the bringing together of many skills.

Maps from play

To help develop these skills, start from play and begin to develop graphicacy work using toys (the train set, farm animals, sand tray, LEGO). Provide the children with opportunities to make and use maps or plans (for instance of the train lay-out) For example, they could make a farmyard in the sand tray with animals. They are laying out the plan of a farm as they do so. They could then draw what they have done. Expect their early attempts to be very simple. Children need repeated opportunities to develop their graphicacy skills.

Unifix construction

Give children approximately six cubes with which to make a Unifix construction. Ask them to record their model as a diagram or 'map', in such a way that other children could replicate it – to make assembly instructions for other children. This sets challenges like *How do you indicate one cube above another?*

Weather recording

● Discuss the weather each day so that the children can practise and expand their weather vocabulary. Begin with formal observations (for example, recording relative temperature, sun, wind direction and strength, rain, cloud) and keep a weekly chart. Introduce formal and standard measures, using thermometers to record air, ground and water temperatures as appropriate. (You can make your own weather-recording instruments as part of design and technology, then use them for geography.) Allow the children to invent their own symbols for recording the daily weather before you introduce conventional weather symbols. At the end of the week compare one week with the previous week.

● Extend the weather chart to include columns for: Playtime (in or out)... Clothes worn (for outside play). The children can fill in the chart for each playtime, morning, lunchtime and afternoon. At the end of a week or fortnight look for a pattern.

● Keep a chart with columns for temperature and wind direction and again look for patterns (*Is it colder when the wind is from the north than when it is from the south? How do playground shadows relate to the time of day/*

position of the sun? When it rains is the wind usually from the same direction? Does rainwater draining down a slope always follow the same route?)

Fieldwork records

Using a variety of pictorial forms, record fieldwork walks and journeys undertaken by the class around school and in the local area. These could extend from individual drawings and pictorial maps to large-scale wall displays. Show the children a real map and mark their route on it to help them appreciate its length, shape, and direction relative to school.

School model

Create model classrooms using small painted boxes. Label them appropriately then use them to make a model of the school by placing them on an outline plan of the school (painted on an old sheet for easy storage). Encourage children to identify features on the model, record the model in pictorial forms; record as plans.

Street model

Use painted boxes to represent houses or shops (pictorially or you could use just name labels). Place them correctly (location, sequence) on a street plan (again painted on an old sheet). Consider ground floor land-use and above ground usage. Place coloured stickers on the boxes with each colour representing the use of the building (house, shop, pub, school, church). *Which is the dominant colour, therefore the dominant building type?* Transfer the information from the model (3-D) to a map (2-D).

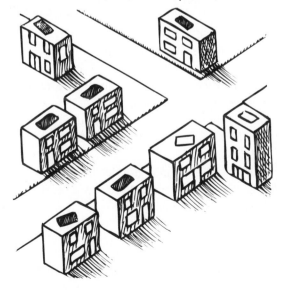

Land-use map

Make a simple land-use map of the locality of the school. Walk round the area to enable the children to identify the categories needed (the previous model-making activity should help). When you have established which categories will be included, give each one a number. Walk round the area again, this time recording the information in numerical form on a map. Back in the classroom, convert the numerical data to colour-coded information and include a key to remind everyone what the colours mean. Analyse the map for patterns such as houses in one group, shops in a row and so on.

Story geography

Develop geography from stories by asking geographical questions. Encourage children to imagine the spatial relationships within the story and to represent them as pictorial maps.

Quality of environment study

The school grounds are a good environment in which to carry out a practical 'quality of the environment' study, providing opportunities to 'observe, **question** and **record**, and to **communicate** ideas and information'. Begin by asking some general questions. *What do you like and dislike about this environment? What do you find attractive or unattractive? Why? What makes a part of the playground 'nice' or 'nasty'? How can the playground be improved? By whom? Can the improvement be maintained?*

Introduce ideas of individual and collective responsibility.
You might also like to introduce the collection and recording of data in the following ways:
▶ Divide the school grounds into areas or zones and record these on a large plan.
▶ Identify 'good' and 'bad' points about each.

Assessment

What do the children know? Consider this particularly in terms of geographical vocabulary used appropriately to label and describe physical and human features of place; about the local area, the contrasting locality, the wider world.

What can they do? Look for children's ability to way-find around the school, their use of geographical skills, the resources they can use to find information, their ability to ask and respond to geographical questions, give opinions, make comparisons and offer explanations.

What have they experienced? Look at the topics, activities, fieldwork (experiences outside the classroom) you have covered with the class.

How have they demonstrated their knowledge? Look for evidence through talk, drawing, map-making, writing and practical activities (sorting, matching, sequencing).

What are they working towards? What is the next conceptual, skills or enquiry stage?

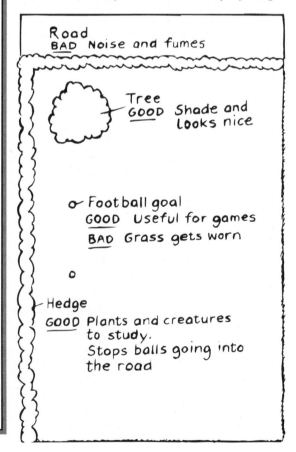

Music

Your first task is to find out what has already been experienced and learned by your class so you can plan what you want to teach them in Year 2. There will always be a need in the teaching of music for recapitulation of earlier experiences, in order to reinforce the ideas explored at earlier stages. Most of the work done in the reception class and Year 1 will have been to explore sounds in as many ways as possible. One of the main activities in Year 2 will be to use those sounds and to create simple pieces of music. The National Curriculum puts it this way:

Pupils recognise and explore how sounds can be organised. They sing with a sense of the shape of the melody, and perform simple patterns and accompaniments keeping to a steady pulse. They choose carefully and order sounds within simple structures such as beginning, middle, end, and in response to given starting points. They represent sounds with symbols and recognise how the musical elements can be used to create different moods and effects. They improve their own work.

The children will be singing a wider repertoire of songs, be working in small groups (pairs or groups of three to five children). They will have more of an opinion of the kinds of music they like and dislike and should be beginning to describe some of their music, and that of others, using a few of the recognised musical terms.

They will also begin to create symbols to record their music in graphic notation. All of their work should be more structured than at earlier levels. This should all lead towards a greater understanding of the music of others as well as their own.

At all levels, music should be seen as part of the whole school curriculum, to be well integrated with other subjects, but to have an identity of its own.

Music

Key areas: Performing, composing, listening, appraising

A curriculum for music-making will always ask for sounds to be explored through performing and composing, listening and appraising, and at times it is useful to look at the areas separately. However, in a successful music session, all four areas are in action at the same time. A music-maker will listen to sounds, discuss them, choose appropriate ones to place together in some order, move them around and then will perform with them. This is no less true in Year 2 than it is at university and should be encouraged at all times. These skills are involved in all the activities suggested over the next few pages.

The activities listed will explore the elements of music: *Pitch* (high/low) *Duration* (long/short) *Dynamics* (loud/quiet/silence) *Tempo* (fast/slow) *Timbre* (quality of sounds – tinkling/rattling/smooth/ringing) *Texture* (one or more sounds) and *Structure* (building a piece of music).

A music session, often very enjoyable, can sometimes lack purpose, for example: *Shall we sing this round? Who wants to play on the instruments today? Make up some music with your friends. Dance to this music.* If you are aware of the musical elements, and direct a session towards their exploration, the session becomes more focused, interesting and appropriate.

What should they be able to do?
Key area: Pitch

By Year 2, you should be able to assume that all the children will have explored the sounds of high and low by listening to sounds in the environment and exploring their own vocal sounds, and have some knowledge of how a high sound and a low sound can be made on a tuned instrument. Since this is vital to music-making, these ideas should be reinforced at the beginning of the year so that they can be used later.

To make high and low sounds on an instrument, it is necessary to have a pitched instrument (such as a xylophone, glockenspiel, chime bars, metallophone, recorders, hand bells, violin, piano) since you cannot hear a real difference of high and low on untuned percussion. It is important to have some of these instruments available for the children to work with in Year 2 so that they can experience playing 'simple pieces and accompaniments' and 'make expressive use of the musical element' (pitch) as suggested in the National Curriculum for Music.

These instruments are expensive. Use this as a time to reinforce the fact that musical instruments are not toys, but valuable pieces of equipment to be respected and cared for. Children should learn to replace the bars and notes in the correct order (CDEFGABC) on tuned percussion instruments (glockenspiels, xylophones, metallaphones) at the end of a session. The instruments should be available whenever possible, along with untuned instruments, for individual explorations (placing them on a music table where children can have access to them would be ideal).

High and low sounds, both vocal and instrumental should be being used in small groups (pairs/groups of three to five) by the end of the year. The short pieces created should involve some kind of simple structure (repetition/questions and answers). The children should be able to discuss their high/low music with others and should have listened to how composers have used high and low sounds in their music. They should have explored graphic notation and found ways to record high and low sounds.

Key area: Duration

Making long and short sounds will have been thoroughly explored earlier, now it is time to use these sounds. The children should have begun to find a regular beat in a piece of music – clapping to it, marching to it, moving to it. This is like the constant tick of a clock that you can be aware of even if you cannot hear it. The children should be attempting to identify a regular beat in their songs and dances and be responding to it. During Year 2, introduce simple rhythms that can fit with the beat. A song might be sung with lots of different length notes in it, both fast and slow (for example, 'He's Got the Whole World in His Hands'), but the children should still be able to clap a steady beat while singing (1 2 3 4).

The use of body percussion is an interesting way of keeping a pulse/beat going and adding a different rhythm. The children should also experiment with this idea on their instruments, both untuned and tuned. By the end of the year, most of them should be creating short pieces of music using a constant beat or simple rhythms, sometimes together. They should be talking about their work and improving it as a result of the discussions. They will also have listened to a variety of recorded pieces, responded to the beat through actions, movement or dance and be able to say if the sounds were long or short.

Key area: Dynamics

In Year 2, children should be beginning to learn how composers use **dynamics**. They will already have spent much time exploring loud and soft sounds and how these can be changed and have listened for these sounds in the environment. Once there has been some recapitulation of these ideas, then the dynamics can be used in their own compositions. By the end of the year, most children should know the symbols used for soft (piano, p) loud (forte, f) getting louder (crescendo, <) and getting softer (diminuendo, >). These can be introduced in a variety of ways: through flash cards, through games and by looking for them in other people's music (song books and hymn books, for example). They should be able to understand, use and control the sounds p and f in response to the symbols in their own music and that of others. They should be able to work together in pairs, small groups and as a class and be responsive to the dynamics of a piece. There are examples of dynamics in all pieces of music, though some have greater contrasts than others, and the children should be listening and recognising these.

Key area: Tempo

In the two previous years, children will have simply explored fast and slow sounds within their own environment. In Year 2, they should be being introduced to the way in which **tempo** (speed) can affect the music they create and how it is used in the music they listen to. Tempo can reflect the whole mood of a piece of music. The funeral march cannot be played at a fast speed and create the required effect any more than 'The Flight of the Bumble Bee' can be played slowly to achieve its effect.

The children should have heard how composers use tempo for effect and be copying the ideas in their own music. They will be aware of the tempo of songs by copying you, but on occasions it would be useful to discuss why the composer asks, at the beginning of a song, for a certain speed. In their own music making they should be encouraged to use a variety of speeds when composing with the voice or using body percussion or instruments. Pieces such as a 'Slow/Fast/Slow' piece or the 'Hare and the Tortoise' can be most effective.

Key area: Timbre

Timbre can be a fascinating element to explore but it requires some listening with concentration. As the children grow older, they should be able to listen for more specific sounds and discover the timbre of voices and instruments. By the end of the year most children should easily recognise the differences between 'tinkling, rattling, smooth, ringing' sounds as suggested in the National Curriculum, and should be able to make these sounds and to group instruments in these sound groups. They should also have looked at how these sounds can be used as musical descriptions (rattling bones, tinkling water, smooth rainbows, ringing bells) and how they might affect a mood (tinkling – happy, rattling – uncomfortable, smooth – calm, ringing – bright).

The children should also have used timbre to create effects (excitement, dullness, fear, celebration). By the end of the year, they should have listened to a variety of recorded pieces with timbre in mind as a point of focus.

Key area: Texture

By the end of Year 2, the children should have sung and played both as soloists and in small groups, as well as with the whole class group. They will therefore have experienced **texture** in music. As the children move through this stage, they will be beginning to use the textures they are most comfortable with. They should have tried different combinations of voices and instruments. They should have had opportunities to contrast sounds in questions and answers (voices, many voices, voices, many voices) in the manner of the working songs of the past, many Negro spirituals and even today's car songs. There should have been much discussion about combinations of sounds: *Do you really like those two sounds together? Why? Why not?* or *Try playing this chime bar (E) with this one (G). Do you like the sound? Now ask a friend to add another one (B). What do you think of that combination?* By the end of the year the children will be becoming more adventurous in their choice of combinations of sound.

Key area: Structure

As children begin to understand more about the elements of music, provide more tools for them to use in their own compositions. They will find composing even the simplest piece of music so much easier if they also have a definite **structure** to work with. As they begin Year 2, most children will be just beginning to place their sounds in a structured form. The easiest form to follow will be that of repetition: choosing a few sounds, putting them together and repeating the pattern. They will have experienced this in songs (such as 'Old Macdonald') and in some of the 'Copy me' games played at an earlier stage. During the year, encourage them to make up short musical phrases for voice, body percussion or instruments and to use repetition to create a piece of music. This can be done by using one or more of the elements. By the end of the year most of them should have progressed to developing longer groups of contrasting sounds and placing them in a beginning/middle/end structure.

Another easy structure to use is the sandwich structure of A/B/A or Ternary Form. The children should be able to create a tune, change it and then play the first tune again to finish the piece. All the elements can be used and this gives scope for every child to display his or her musical knowledge. Some children should also be playing simple instrumental accompaniments (repeated notes, sound effects) to songs, stories, poetry and dance.

Practical ideas

The easiest way of involving all the children in musical activities is to make sure you can see them and they can see you. Sit them in a circle whenever possible, insist on silence while you give out your instructions and make sure you have eye contact with them all. The activities should be very short and should change frequently. Alternate singing activities with creating and listening activities and a movement activity whenever possible.

Making a start

● Play a tape of a new song. *Who can remember the words or the music of the first line?* Listen again and ask the children to try to remember another line.

● Pass a single note around a circle. *Can you copy in turn the note I sing?* Change the note when it reaches you again. Let a child start the note, too.

● Find out what the children's favourite songs are. Agree on hand movements to signal quiet singing (hand closed), loud singing (hand open), getting louder (hand opening), and getting softer (hand closing), and sing the songs, varying the sounds by using the hand signals. Allow a child to be a conductor whenever possible.

● Clap a rhythm pattern then ask the children to copy it. Change the pattern often and occasionally ask a child to be a leader. The copying should sound like echoes.

● Ask the children to play just the rhythm, not the tune, of a nursery rhyme on a tuned or untuned percussion instrument. Let each child have a try. Can the rest of the class recognise the rhyme?

Introducing key areas

Breathing

● Play 'Copy me' by asking the children to follow your breathing. Take big, deep, audible breaths and ask them to copy you. Can they keep in time with you? Change the breaths so they are longer. How long can the children hold their breath?

● Sing well-known songs and ask the children to try to sing a whole line without taking a new breath.

Song strategies

● Find some question and answer songs to sing, using either a soloist and a larger group or two groups of singers (for example, 'Who Killed Cock Robin?' 'Where Are You Going to, My Pretty Maid?' 'What Shall We Do with the Drunken Sailor?' 'There's a Hole in My Bucket'). Choose the more confident singers to be the soloists.

● Ask the children to make up question and answer songs in pairs.

● Take two notes (G and E) and play them repeatedly to the children. Ask them to make up name songs/skipping songs/playground songs just using the two notes. This could be done in small groups or in pairs. Ask the children to share their new songs with the class.

● Sing songs that can have very simple accompaniments. There are many good publications which include these and do not

Music

expect knowledge of notation. They suggest two-note accompaniments or rhythmic accompaniments on untuned percussion. *Flying a Round: 88 round and partner songs*, chosen by David Gadby and Beatrice Harrop (A & C Black) and *Gently into Music,* Mary York, (Longman) are particularly useful publications. Ask a small group of children to practise the accompaniment, then to play to the class. Have a performance with the group accompanying the singing.

● Rehearse together as a class, trying to follow a conductor and keeping together. Then sing to another group of children or in an assembly.

Body percussion

● Ask the children to play 'Copy me' as you keep a regular beat, tapping quietly with your toes. Now add a different rhythm either by hand clapping, knee slapping or finger clicking. *Can you keep the two sounds going at the same time?*

● Play 'Question and Answers' by using the body as an instrument. Clap a short, easy-to-remember pattern. Ask the children to answer with a pattern of the same length but a little different. (This works better if you ask individual children to respond rather than the whole class.) *Can you make it sound like an answer to my question?*

Instruments

● Introduce the children to the tuned percussion instruments you have in the classroom. To begin with only introduce a few instruments at a time. These could be placed in the centre of the circle and be used when needed by just a few children. A 'Copy me' activity is a good way to begin. As the children become more used to the instruments, gradually work towards everyone having one to make specific sounds until all the children are working in pairs and small groups with a selection of instruments.

Try to have a variety of instruments rather than too many of the same type so that you have variation in sounds. There are also many different kinds of hard and soft beaters made in a variety of materials, such as felt, rubber, wood and plastic. Try to obtain a collection of different beaters and let the children experiment with them. Encourage them to become aware of the wide range of different sounds that they make.

● It can be interesting to change the sounds of instruments. Different beaters will make different sounds, but there are other things the children can do. If they hold the bar of a glockenspiel while playing, the sound will not be able to ring. It will sound dampened. A chime bar can be struck on the bar with a beater in one hand, while a piece of card can be wobbled just above the hole. This makes a lovely sound. Holding the skin of a drum or a tambourine while the instrument is hit will also make a new sound. Ask the children to experiment with the instruments and create new sounds to be used later in their pieces.

● Find a picture that contains a variety of sound suggestions. Ask the children to tell you what they would hear if they were inside that picture. (A train coming through the trees, smoke puffing from the chimney, trees waving in the breeze, birds overhead, wheels clattering on the line... .) Discuss which instruments might be appropriate for each sound. Try different instruments and ask the children in which order the sounds might come. Build up a picture, sound on sound.

● Organise the children into pairs and give each partner an instrument. One instrument can be tuned, the other untuned. Ask the children to make up a 'musical sandwich'. The first child plays a short pattern, then the second child plays a new pattern. The first child then plays his or her pattern again. Invite each pair to play their sandwich to the class (ABA structure).

● Use silence for effect by asking small groups of children to make up a piece of music entitled 'The Dark Night'. Explain that it must include long, low sounds, short, high-pitched sounds, and silence. They should first try to create this picture using only voices but could then move on to using instruments. Make sure everyone has a chance to perform their pieces.

Writing it down

Use every opportunity to encourage the children to record all their music in graphic notation and to keep a music folder of their scores. Explain that they need to keep a record so that they can pass the music on for other people to play, in the same way that composers have always handed down their music. They only need to use simple graphic symbols: * could be a clap, ^ could be a knee slap, ~ could be a click and – a stamp. Allow the children to choose their own symbols and make sure they include a key to the symbols on the music.

Recording of music composed on tuned percussion instruments can be done at this stage by using the letter names of the notes (CDEFGABC). Short notes are placed closer together than longer notes (CDC   F). It is never too early for children to try to write down their compositions and children enjoy creating their own simple form of notation. Allow them to take the instrument to a quiet corner where a friend cannot hear them, pick out a tune they know, write the letter notation and then give it to the friend. *Can he/she play and name the tune?* Encourage the use of a tape recorder so that children can play back their compositions.

Tonic solfa

● If you know the hand signs for tonic solfa (see illustration), show the children the signs that are used for soh (G) and me (E). As you change your hand positions, can they sing the new note?

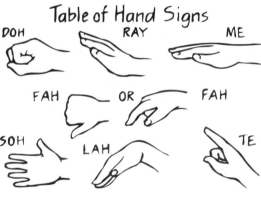

Table of Hand Signs

● Make up short patterns in solfa, (s————ss m m s————ss m) with everyone trying to sing while making the signs. Explain to the children that, in the past, all children learnt to sing and to read music by using this sign language.

● Sing 'Doh a Deer' from *The Sound of Music.*

Developing key areas

Voices

At every opportunity, sing with the children. If you are confident, then let the children copy you as you sing new songs. If you feel happier with help, then find good tape recordings of appropriate songs and use them frequently. There are some excellent tapes available. (Borrow some from friends or the library in order to find ones you like before buying any.) Repetition is the key to success at this stage, so find the children's favourite songs and keep singing them. Actions also help songs along so, whenever possible, add appropriate movements. Always encourage shy children to join in with you. Ask a best friend to sing along with them, or place them next to a confident singer. Use a toy microphone to encourage shy singers or children with speech difficulties to join in. Discourage shouters or poor singers by asking them to listen to others and then to join in again. Everyone can sing, all that is needed is plenty of practice.

● Divide the class into two groups and sing simple rounds in two parts (see *Flying a Round,* A & C Black). Do not attempt to sing a song as a round until everyone can sing the tune. Have some keen singers in each group.

Names and rhythms

● Ask the children to sit in a circle. Each child, in turn should be able to clap the rhythm of their name. Some will clap once (Bryn), some twice (Karen) some three times (Shazadan).

● Play a name game using name clapping. Organise the children into a circle. Make sure there is one chair short in the circle. The child without a chair stands in the centre of the circle. He/she claps once, twice or three times. All the children whose name would fit that rhythm get up and change seats, while the spare child nips into a chair. The child who is leftover claps for another changeover, and so on.

● Choose the names of four famous London places. These might be Bank, Fleet Street, Ken-sing-ton High Street, Char-ing Cross. Divide the class into four groups and give each group a street name. Practise the sound and how to clap the name with each group. (There can be different interpretations – choose one and stick to it!) Begin with *Bank / / / , Bank / / / ,* keeping silent in the / / / , then add Fleet Street (*Fleet Street / /).* When the sounds of these two fit together, add a third name, then a fourth. This will take some practise but is fun. Then try local street names.

● Ask the children the names of their favourite television programmes. Write a few on the board. Clap the rhythm of these names together. Ask a child to choose one of the names and tap the rhythm out on the shoulder or knee of the nearest child who must pass the rhythm on. Continue for a little while, then ask the last child what the television programme is.

Body percussion

● Design some flash cards to represent the sounds you make (for example, clap *, click ~, stamp – , knee slap ^). Ask the children to respond to the symbols with sounds as you show the cards. Give a selection of the flash cards to smaller groups of children. *Can you use these signs to create a short body percussion piece? Can you write it down, using the signs, for another group to try?*

● Make a storm. Sit in a circle. Begin by rubbing your hands together to make a drizzling sound. The child on your right follows you, then the next child, and so on in turn round the circle. When the child on your left starts hand-rubbing, you switch to tapping your fingers on your palm to make light raindrops. This goes round the circle again, but no-one must start the new sound till it reaches their neighbour. Then knee-slapping follows for heavier rain, soft stamping feet for distant thunder, louder stamping for increasing thunder and a few big double stamps for extra loud thunder. The sounds are repeated in reverse order as the storm dies away.

Action songs

● Try singing a song with actions while another group is singing with different actions. 'First You Make Your Fingers Click' from *Flying a Round* (A & C Black) is a good round to try.

● Make up a song to the tune of 'Frere Jacques' ('I Hear Thunder') with actions. It might be:
I am clapping I am clapping,
Slap my knees, slap my knees,
Tap my toes so lightly, tap my toes so lightly,
Click with ease, click with ease.

● The children could try making up other action songs using different well-known tunes.

Music to act to

● Ask the children to make groups of three. Each group should have one instrument (untuned), a player and two actors. Provide a choice of titles for them to act out and accompany with music. The titles could be 'The quarrel', 'The gossips', 'The tin man', 'The baby'. Ask each trio to perform to the whole group.

● The children will need to work in groups of four for this activity. Two find appropriate instruments and two move. Suggest titles such as 'Fast and slow' or 'The hare and the tortoise'. Ask each group to create a piece of music with movement to describe the title. Each section can be very short, but it must be in the 'fast/slow/fast' or 'slow/fast/slow' pattern.

Animal music

● Invite the children to tell you about their favourite animals. *What sounds do they make? Are they high/low, short/long, soft/loud sounds?* Stand in the centre of the circle of children and point to any child to make his/her animal sound. Move quickly from one child to another at random. Sometimes point to two people. This is your animal orchestra. The children will need to keep an eye on you as the conductor. Let the children take turns at being the conductor, too.

Listening together

● In Year 2 the children should be listening to slightly longer pieces of recorded music than before. Make sure that you give them a specific sound to listen for and ask for a response when they hear it. They will hear repetition at the beginning of 'Mars' from the *Planets Suite* by Holst; repeated choruses in most of the songs in the popular charts; gradual crescendo in 'Bolero' by Ravel; clock beats in Leroy Anderson's 'The Syncopated Clock'; sliding sounds in the Prelude from Kodaly's *Hary Janos Suite*. Listen first to your chosen piece of music and decide what it is you would like the children to focus on.

● Listen to 'The Tortoise' from *The Carnival of Animals* (Saint Saëns) to hear how the composer uses slow tempo for effect. Then listen to 'Quick animals'. Use the available instruments, in pairs, to create pieces of contrasting music; one child can play a tortoise, the other a quick animal.

● Play the 'Peter' tune from *Peter and the Wolf* (Prokofiev). *Do you feel happy or sad? Calm or worried?* Play the 'Wolf' music and ask, *How do you feel now?* Working in small groups with a variety of instruments, ask the children first to make happy sounds (short, high, quick) and then to try worried sounds (long, low, silences). Listen to the 'Peter' and the 'Wolf' themes again.

● 'Zip-a-dee doo dah' from Walt Disney's *Song of the South* is a lovely example of a repeating tune. Listen and sing together.

A favourite instrument

● Invite a willing parent, friend or peripatetic instrumental teacher to join you for a music session to talk about their instrument and play it. Let the children ask questions about the instrument, try it, and discuss which instrument they might like to play and why.

Music for assembly

● 'Who Built the Ark?' (from *Someone's Singing, Lord*, A & C Black) is a useful song to work with, bringing many musical elements together. Teach the song, line by line, starting on the note G. Divide the class into two groups and let them sing question and answer. Invite four or five children to play a simple accompaniment on the note G only. They might take the rhythm of one line 'No-ah, No-ah' and play it as an ostinato (repeated tune). Ask small groups of children to use untuned percussion instruments to create sounds to accompany the last line of each verse: 'Hippopotamus, kangaroo, elephant, black roosters, black hens'. It is a very easy tune and

some children might like to work it out for themselves on a xylophone.

This music making could be linked with an animal project, or the story of Noah. Listen to 'Captain Noah and His Floating Zoo' by Joseph Horovitz and Michael Flanders and then create musical animal portraits.

● Use every opportunity to let the class or small groups of children perform to the rest of the school. Whenever a child or a group creates a pleasing piece, invite them to talk about it, describe how they made it and then play it.

● Some children may be having music lessons – encourage them to perform in assemblies either as soloists or accompanying the singing.

Ideas bank

● Encourage the children to write stories which will lend themselves to accompanying sounds.

● Ask the children to create a story from a picture, and then to choose instruments that represent the mood of that picture to use as a background to the story. Some of these instrument sounds could be taped.

● Find some poems that include many allusions to sounds (for instance 'Seashell' by Enid Madoc Jones). Encourage the children to make up their own. Then ask them to make up quiet, background sounds which will create an appropriate atmosphere when played as the poems are read.

● Make a collection of milk bottles or jam jars. Fill each to a different level with water. The children can experiment by hitting the side of the bottle with a beater to see what sound is produced. *How can you make that sound higher or lower? Put the bottles in order – low on the left and high on the right. Can you play tunes on them?*

● Tie different lengths of metal strips on to string and hang them up as wind chimes. They will make very pleasant random sounds.

● Collect clay plant pots of different sizes. Hang them up and play them with a hard beater.

Assessment

The most important outcome of music making with young children is that they should have enjoyed it. This will be extremely obvious at the end of any music session since children will want to sing, dance, clap, move on the way to their next activity. However, there are other things that can be noted to help you evaluate whether or not you have achieved what you set out to do. The most important things for you to do in making music are to:
- get the children involved and encourage them to listen;
- allow them to perform;
- ask them what they think;
- give them lots of opportunities to create musical sounds and to put them together.

What can they do?

Use this checklist to see what they have learned. Can they:
- Listen attentively to sounds?
- Collect sounds?
- Recognise some differences of sounds?
- Re-create sounds?
- Use sounds in a more structured way?
- Respond to sounds?
- Discuss sounds?
- Sing a variety of songs?
- Play simple pieces of music on tuned and untuned instruments?
- Play simple accompaniments?
- Demonstrate an increasing awareness of pulse/beat?
- Listen to short pieces of music?
- Discuss their own music using simple musical terms and suggest improvements?
- Use a simple form of graphic notation?

What have they experienced?

Have the children:
- Explored sounds both vocal and instrumental?
- Used their body as an instrument to make sounds?
- Handled and used tuned and untuned percussion instruments?
- Responded to music through dance and movement?
- Worked in small groups and as a whole class?
- Used the musical elements in their work?
- Gained some musical confidence?
- Used a tape recorder and recorded their own work?

Can they perform?

Whenever possible, encourage the children to perform. A class assembly presented to other children is a good way of sharing music-making. Invite parents, carers, friends and peripatetic music teachers, to join in a music session and to make music together.

Art and Design

This year builds on the things which the children have explored and experienced in Year 1. The criteria for Knowledge, skills and understanding in the National Curriculum provide a firm foundation for art and design at Key Stage 1.

You should help your class to develop their visual perception, and the skills that are needed for investigation and making. The children should have opportunities to:

● record responses to both the made and the natural environment;
● gather and use resources and materials;
● use a range of materials and techniques;
● review and modify their work.

Give them opportunities to develop knowledge and understanding of the work of artists, designers and craftspeople and to evaluate art, craft and design.

What should they be able to do?

In Year 2 most children will have a developing visual vocabulary of marks and shapes. The need to repeat images will not be as apparent as in Year 1 but experimentation and practice in the use of tools and materials continues to be fundamental.

Children in Year 2 will have noticeably stronger likes and dislikes than in Year 1. They will have begun to find a personal style and way of communicating in both two and three dimensions. It is important to appreciate each child's response, recognising that not all children will work in the same way. Personal imagery should be respected, strengths should be recognised and opportunities given for further growth and development. Some children, towards the end of Year 2, will want to be able to create a likeness.

Children at this stage will be able to work from observation as well as memory. They will be responsive visually to stories and events and will be keen to use their imagination.

Most children, hopefully, will have: had experience of a range of graphic materials; used thick paint and watercolour; made prints using found objects; been introduced to collage; modelled with materials in three dimensions. Experiences in Year 2 should include:

● developing experience of familiar tools and materials, and introducing new ones;
● continued work in the use of the visual elements which are the building blocks of art: pattern, texture, colour, line, tone, shape, form, space;
● visual communication and expression, using personal ideas and work from the imagination stimulated by visits, events, stories, music, and so on;
● a range of developing skills relating to the techniques of drawing, painting, printing, collage, fabric work and work in three dimensions;
● introduction to narrative and use of the imagination in the work of other artists, craftspeople and designers including at least one example from a non-western culture.

Practical ideas

Working through the senses, particularly sight and touch, is of vital importance at all stages of education. Visual and tactile skills can be developed through increased opportunities to work from observation of real and interesting things brought into the classroom, or through taking children outside to experience a place of visual or historical interest, either locally or further afield. Asking open-ended questions and discussing what they have seen and discovered stimulates interest and provides ideas and starting points.

Give the children opportunities to research images and ideas from a collection of related books and videos so that they are informed and made aware through a variety of resources.

Allow starting points occasionally to be initiated by the children, perhaps triggered by a favourite story or character, an exciting object, or an important family event or happening. Give them the opportunity to work freely from their own ideas and imagination.

In addition to working as a whole class, they should also sometimes work in pairs, small groups or individually.

Using knowledge and experience which they have gained in earlier years, the children should make choices and decisions about materials and the way in which they will respond to a challenge in two or three dimensions.

If pupils have not already had the opportunity, now is the time to introduce simple graphics and painting computer software as another means of drawing, creating and changing patterns and exploring alternative combinations of colour.

 ## Making a start

A well-organised environment

The whole classroom environment, from the pictures on the walls to the way in which the tools and materials are arranged and cared for, is part of the display and is a statement about the way in which the children's work is viewed and valued. This is a significant part of the teaching and, in Year 2, children can assume some responsibility for organising and maintaining the materials for art, craft and design.

A lively and rich learning environment, where collections of visually exciting and tactile objects are brought in by you and the children, will stimulate curiosity and encourage an interest in, and response to, the world around them. Written comments can usefully accompany the displays, particularly if they are presented in the form of a task or challenge.

It is important that some displays are of work in three dimensions so aim for the children to produce some such work during this year.

Tools and materials

Provide good quality tools and materials and remind children of the need to care for them. Brushes should be washed and stored with the bristles uppermost. Glue-spreaders should be stored away from the brushes. Water is best

offered in shallow containers which are not easily knocked over. Paint, especially in readymix pots, can be quite an attractive feature if kept clean and stored tidily. Plastic sweet jars make good storage for coloured threads and small collage materials. The children can sort threads into colour families. They can also be involved in sorting fabrics into small open plastic storage trays for future use in collage work or stitching activities. Flat trays also make good storage for water-colour boxes, packets of crayons or oil pastels.

Artefacts as sources of ideas

As far as possible it is good for the children to be encouraged to bring interesting objects and artefacts into the classroom as this gives them a feeling of ownership. Additionally, collections of interesting items and artefacts can sometimes be borrowed from museums. These may relate specifically to a topic or theme and can be useful for extending children's experience.

Through discussion, using open-ended questions, you can begin to help the children to discover the potential of images and artefacts and collections as a source of ideas for their own work. If it is a picture, discuss the colours, the way the artist has worked, the mood and what is happening. If it is an artefact, ask them to look at the shape, colour and pattern. If it is not valuable, allow them to handle the object and encourage them to describe the texture. Initial responses can be recorded in a sketchbook using words and drawings. The children could then respond by creating a painting, drawing, print or collage, or by making something similar using clay or junk materials.

Themes

In Year 2 explore themes relating to the children and other people. For example subjects such as figures real and imagined, the world around, houses and homes, animals, flowers, vehicles and machines are all still of interest. The seasons are a good starting point for natural forms as children can find and bring in examples for themselves.

There are many projects which can be interpreted purely for art, or in a cross-curricular manner, in which factual and creative writing, prose and poetry, drama, movement, mathematics, and so on can all play a role. Examples offering potential for this age-group could be:

● Homes: look at paintings with buildings – *What kind of person lived there?* Look at Van Gogh's painting of his bedroom, Pre-Raphaelite interiors, Dutch interiors, paintings of the inside of his house by the French artist Bonnard, paintings of historical houses, Lowry, Indian art, Persian art, and so on.

● Growing things and gardens: look at the

paintings by Monet of his garden at Giverny, Van Gogh's 'Sunflowers' and his paintings of irises, the close-up paintings of flowers by Giorgia O'Keefe and possibly botanical paintings.

These themes are followed through in the suggested work below.

Making a start

Exploring and developing ideas

Expressive work based on real or imagined experiences and work from memory and imagination should be offered in Year 2. Stories, music and drama are all good starting points, and individual responses and ideas should be encouraged and shared.

Observational work from both natural and manufactured forms and environments should be developed, for example, looking at pebbles, shells, feathers and other natural forms brought in by you or by a child, or a collection of jugs or pots of different shapes and forms.

Investigating and making art, craft and design

Exploring what the tools and materials will do, sometimes through trial and error, and sometimes through guided discovery, combining materials and overlaying them, is an essential part of the art experience at all stages in children's development and should be recognised and accepted as part of the process. You will also need

to teach specific techniques.

Drawing

By Year 1, children will have had experience of the range of marks made with soft drawing pencils. In Year 2 you can also introduce the use of charcoal. Provide short sticks of charcoal as long pieces will break. Work on small pieces of paper at first so that children get used to the feel of the material. Some children find charcoal messy but persevere, hands can always be washed. Challenge them to see how many greys and blacks they can make. Ask them to make two marks close together. *Can you make the marks touch by rubbing them?* Immediately afterwards, ask them to do a drawing which gives a good opportunity for blending, for example a windy day or a furry animal.

Painting

● Now is the time to build on earlier experiences and, in particular, to offer further experience of colour mixing. For the suggested Homes theme, children could design their own ideal bedroom.

▶ Show them a reproduction of Van Gogh's painting of his bedroom. Discuss the colours that Van Gogh used. Ask: *Why do you think he chose them? Do you like them? What colours would you choose?*

Provide a range of paint and brushes. Suggest that they design their bedroom in their sketchbooks first. They can also use their

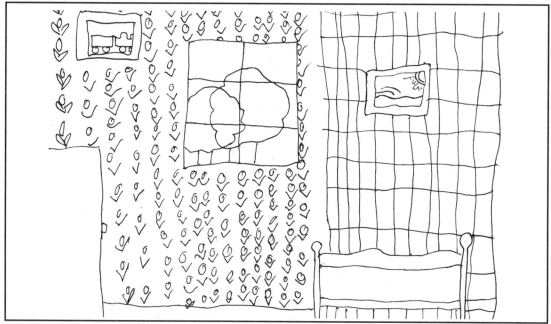

sketchbooks to experiment with mixing colours for the walls, bedcover, curtains, and so on. Spend some time discussing the results and choices for the final picture.

● For the Growing Things theme you could paint gardens. Show the children pictures painted by Monet of his garden in Giverney or other painting of gardens that are available to you. You may like to read the story of a little girl who visits Monet's garden (*Linnea in Monet's Garden* by Christine Bjork).

Printing

Show the children some examples of printed wallpapers (they may also be able to bring in some examples themselves). Discuss repeating patterns – this could link with work in maths – and ask the children to print their own wallpaper for a model house (see below). Provide paper, small wooden blocks, or cut vegetables to print with, or allow them to use objects of their choice. You will also need small plastic trays with a small amount of paint in the middle. Place a piece of flat cleaning sponge (about 1 cm thick) on top of the paint. The children press the objects on top of the sponge. The children should practise in their sketchbooks first before starting on the sheet of 'wallpaper'.

Collage

Cover the tables with newspaper. Provide paper, scissors, glue and spreaders. Use pictures from old home design magazines or similar and talk about selecting images that can be put together in order to create an imaginary room. Try several alternatives before sticking the images down. Encourage the children to talk about the reasons for their choices.

Provide a selection of small pieces of paper of varying colours, patterns and textures and a range of small pieces of interesting fabric. Plastic cutlery trays or plastic sweet jars will encourage organisation of the colours.

The children could also use the collage materials to design a garden. Talk first about the texture and colour of soil, grass, petals, bark, and look closely at flowers, leaves and grasses.

Modelling

Provide opportunities for working with malleable materials such as clay and also for working with paper and card. Ask the children to bring in a box, for example, a shoe box. Turned on its side it can be used as a basis for children's designs for a room or a house. They can use the wallpaper which they printed to decorate the insides of the boxes.

The children can design gardens and then create them in an ice-cream tub or similar container. A sequence of drawings can be made from the gardens as they change and grow. As the 'gardens' would take several sessions to complete, they could be displayed as work in progress alongside the designs and possibly some writing.

Vocabulary

It is important throughout all these key areas that appropriate language is introduced. Words such as *explore, record, observe, imagine, select, identify, respond, describe* should be introduced and used in appropriate contexts. Some of these words can be handwritten or produced on the computer as an integral part of a display. Some of them can be introduced in the context of the children's own and other artists' work, through open-ended questions and discussion, to communicate their opinions and observations.

Explore colours

Offer the three primary colours – red, blue and yellow, plus black and white. You will also need brushes, mixing palettes and small pieces of square cartridge paper or sketchbooks.

▶ *Explore the different kinds of red you can mix.*
▶ Explore ways of making red to match selected items in a collection of red things, for example a tomato, a red pepper, a red toy car, a red sock. *Do you need more than one kind of red?*

Observe and record

Line the inside of a jar with blotting paper and place a runner bean seed between the paper and the side of the jar. Put a little water in the bottom of the jar to keep the blotting paper damp. Watch the bean grow. Provide cartridge paper and pens or soft drawing pencils. Observe and record the bean's growth through a series of drawings. (Make sure the children date them.) Discuss the value of keeping records of something over a period of time. This could be linked, of course, to the story of *Jack and the Beanstalk* and to work in science.

Imagine houses

Show the children pictures of different kinds of houses. Include some from other parts of the world. Try and include pictures of dramatic buildings such as the Sydney Opera House, the Guggenheim Museum in New York or the Museum of Modern Art in Bilbao, the strange buildings of the Spanish architect Gaudi, and so on, to stimulate their imagination. Offer the three primary colours and black and white, hog hair brushes, palettes for mixing, a range of paper, pencils and charcoal. Ask the children to imagine an unusual house of their own and to make a painting or a drawing.

Select and respond

Show reproductions of paintings of houses and homes by a range of artists. Talk about them. Invite the children to respond to the paintings by selecting one that they like or do not like and to give the reasons why.

Sketchbooks

The National Curriculum suggests working with sketchbooks at Key Stage 2 but it is valuable for children to become familiar from the beginning with this way of working. They may have had experience of sketchbooks in Year 1, or possibly news books which are a good starting point from which sketchbooks can be developed. In Year 2, sketchbooks are an ideal place in which to experiment with different tools and materials, to record observations and to develop themes or ideas. (Pieces of plain paper stitched or stapled together with a stronger cover, which the children can then decorate, make a good sketchbook at this stage.)

The elements of art

There should be opportunities for experimentation with the elements of art: line, colour, shape, pattern, texture, form. It is seldom that a work of art has only one element in its make up and children will usually be involved in working with several of the elements in one challenge or project. For example, in connection with the theme of 'growing things' you could introduce the children to the work of the artist Archimboldo who used fruit and leaves to construct heads. Involve the children in:

▶ observational drawings of fruit with pencil – looking at line, tone, pattern, texture and form;

▶ observational drawings of fruit using chalk pastels where they can experiment with blending the pastels to create texture and colour;

▶ observational paintings of fruit to explore colour mixing;

▶ using their sketchbooks to try out various ways of combining fruit to make a face;

▶ creating a final painting or collage.

This is a useful activity for the autumn term when fruit and coloured leaves are plentiful.

Evaluating and developing work

Spend time sitting with the children so that they can talk about and evaluate their own work, finding something positive to say about it. Given opportunities to discuss their work, children will learn to reflect on their work, to modify it and to suggest new ideas. It is also an opportunity to reinforce vocabulary related, for example, to new experiences, elements, tools or techniques.

Display

Display is one of the ways in which children's work can be evaluated.

▶ Involve the children as much as possible in making decisions about the way in which their work is displayed. They can begin to use the computer to make simple labels for the display.

▶ Encourage them to begin to mount their own work.

▶ Try to include everybody's work in the display. Sometimes a 'pavement show', laying out the work on the hall floor, for example, or pinning it up quickly so that it can be celebrated and talked about immediately, is a valuable way of building on the children's experiences and making teaching points while the experience is still fresh in their minds.

Developing key areas

Different artists

Children can be introduced to a range of different artists and to three-dimensional forms. These can be in the form of postcard reproductions collected in a photograph album and situated in the book corner. If you know a lively local artist who would be willing to come into the classroom, this would be a great stimulus. Children can be encouraged to describe a variety of images and artefacts, to voice likes and dislikes and to make choices about which they like best. This can take place through whole-class discussions, group work or spontaneously on an individual basis.

Encourage children to recognise the elements of art in the work of other artists, craftspeople and designers and to apply this knowledge to their own, looking at colour and line in artists' work and responding by using it vigorously in their own work (to express feelings, for example).

Recording from observation and imagination

Approaches

▶ A corner of my bedroom.
▶ A portrait of my friend.
▶ A study of a plant or a shell.
▶ An animal brought into the classroom.
▶ A visit to see local houses or shops.

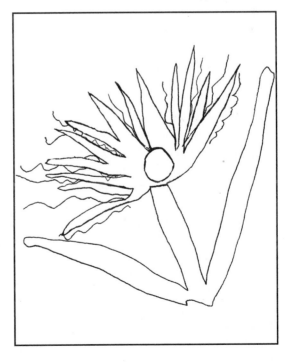

Investigating different kinds of art, craft and design

▶ A collection, for example each child brings in an item from their bedroom.
▶ Taking in something unusual, exciting or surprising, for example an artefact from another country, an unusual fruit or flower.
▶ Taking the children out – perhaps to a building site or special garden.
▶ Finding a story related to your chosen focus.
▶ Using music/songs as extra stimulus.

Observations and comments

▶ *Who does this belong to?*
▶ *Can you tell me what it is?*
▶ *Is it special to you?*
▶ *What shape is it?*
▶ *What colours can you see?*
▶ *Is it rough or smooth?*
▶ *Can you paint a picture of the part of the room where it belongs?*
▶ *Can you paint a picture where the thing you have brought in comes to life?*

Evidence of success

▶ Interest and motivation.
▶ Personal response.
▶ Ability to use descriptive vocabulary.
▶ Memory of room at home.
▶ Ability to use imagination to place the object in a new setting.

Tools, materials and techniques
Approaches

▶ Place the object against a background.
▶ Experiment making different marks with a range of tools.
▶ Experiment with mixing colours and matching.
▶ Use different kinds of materials for example oil pastels, coloured chalks, charcoal.
▶ Offer big and small brushes.
▶ Model the object in clay or Plasticine.

Observations and comments

▶ *What marks can you make with crayon/paint which will look like...?*
▶ *Which tool did you use to make this mark?*
▶ *Which brush can you use to make a tiny/big mark?*
▶ *Which tool/paint are you going to choose to make the...?*

▶ *Which mark do you like best?*
▶ *Why do you like it?*
▶ *Which mark looks like...?*
▶ *Can you mix a different colour?*
▶ *What colours did you use to make your new colour? Can you do it again?*
▶ *Close your eyes and imagine...*

Evidence of success

▶ A willingness to try new things.
▶ Personal response and use of imagination.
▶ Visual and tactile awareness.
▶ Mark-making of all kinds.
▶ Colour mixing and matching.
▶ Awareness of texture.
▶ Involvement and concentration.
▶ Use of appropriate descriptive vocabulary.

Artists, craftspeople and designers
Approaches

▶ Bring in examples or reproductions of a range of art and, if possible, relate these to a chosen theme – buildings, old houses, castles.
▶ Select work showing examples of use of colour, varieties of mark making etc.
▶ Select reproductions of paintings with a narrative content, for example some of the Pre-Raphaelite paintings.
▶ Bring in artefacts from a museum.
▶ Invite a local craftsperson.

Observations and comments

▶ *Which picture do you like best?*
▶ *What colours can you see?*
▶ *What do you think is happening in the picture?*
▶ *What do you think will happen next?*
▶ *Is it a happy/sad picture?*

Evidence of success

▶ Personal likes and dislikes.
▶ Awareness of detail.
▶ Awareness of colour and shape.
▶ Ability to become involved in the content of the picture and be able to project themselves into the story.

Artists from various times and cultures
Approaches

▶ Introduce artefacts from other cultures, for example African and Chinese masks.

▶ Introduce a famous artist, for example the expressive work of Vincent Van Gogh.

Observations and comments
▶ *Do you think this mask is a happy/sad/scary face?*
▶ *Can anybody tell me the name of the country this mask comes from?*
▶ *Has anybody here seen any other masks/work by this artist?*
▶ *Where?*

Evidence of success
▶ An awareness of art in other countries and cultures.
▶ That there are different ways of making and using art and artefacts.
▶ Galleries and museums as places where artists' work can be seen.

Evaluating and developing
Approaches
▶ Looking at different masks – real ones if possible or good illustrations.
▶ Design a mask.
▶ Make masks using strips of paper dipped in non-fungicidal wallpaper paste over a balloon – cover the balloon with Vaseline first and rest it in an ice-cream tub so that it does not roll round.
▶ Experiment with safe natural materials to make 'paint', for example blackberry juice, beetroot juice.
▶ Create a class gallery or museum.

Observations and comments
▶ *What colours can you see?*
▶ *What materials do you think are used to make the 'paint'?*
▶ *What shapes and lines can you see?*
▶ *Which shapes/lines/colours make the mask look scary/happy/sad?*
▶ *Why would someone want to wear a mask?*
▶ *Can you design a mask that you would like to wear or for your friend?*
▶ *What colours/marks/shapes would you use?*

Evidence of success
▶ Observational skills.
▶ Ability to understand the purpose of a mask.
▶ Personal motivation and response.
▶ Ideas for designing a new artefact.
▶ Independent thinking.

Ideas bank
Wall display
The 'unit' approach makes a striking dispay but allows each child to retain part of it afterwards. Each child makes or paints an object or image which is a unit for a large wall or table display, for example, observational paintings of seasonal plants or artefacts. You can restrict the colour depending on the season – for autumn you could offer red, yellow, green, white and black. The children's unit should be of their own devising and sometimes from observation, not from a template which is a poor substitute for lively originality.

Greeting cards
▶ Choose folded pieces of card carefully to get a suitable size/texture.
▶ Encourage children to think of their own ideas or to choose from already completed work, for example, drawings of a member of the family or a family group, a small observational drawing or painting of a single flower or bunch of flowers or a print made from the drawing.
▶ Select a range of tools and materials for the children to choose from. (On occasions, pehaps at Christmas, you might want to restrict the colours offered.)
▶ Use various media – collage, painting, drawing, print.
▶ An image stitched from an observational drawing (a portrait or a house, for example) and mounted on a piece of card with the message underneath can be something a little different.
▶ Encourage children to write their own messages in coloured pen or crayon.
▶ Try attempting something 3-D, for example, a small thumb-pot made from clay makes a little gift. The children can print their own wrapping paper and design gift tags for this or other gifts.

Art and design

Assessment

In Year 2, children's interpretations of what they see may be symbolic but, for some, working in a visually real way will be increasingly important. Encourage both ways of working. They are not mutually exclusive.

It is important to respond sensitively to the questions the children ask, the things they say, what they do and what they give us – whatever stage they are at. However, it is also important to show alternative ways of working.

A vital consideration in any evaluation of outcomes in art is respect for personal and cultural identity, particularly as art should be instrumental in developing self-confidence. It is also important to develop positive attitudes to art through praise, help and encouragement. The beginnings of peer group evaluation are to be encouraged with an emphasis on the importance of positive comments. For example: 'I like the way Amy has used orange next to blue in her picture.' It is possible to evaluate some of the following aspects of the children's art endeavours at this stage:

- How have they used what we have given them?
- What they have done and what they are trying to do?
- What evidence do we see of independent thinking and personal ideas?
- What evidence can we see of developing observational skills?
- Have they been willing to experiment?
- Are they developing a knowledge of how tools and materials behave?
- Have the materials been used in an imaginative way?
- Have they begun to mix colours?
- Have they learned a new skill/technique?
- Are they beginning to understand the context of art, artists, galleries?
- Have they learned about art from another country/culture/period?
- Are they growing more confident?
- Are they motivated and involved?
- Can they work independently/co-operatively?
- Can they talk about their own and each others' work, using appropriate vocabulary, for example?

Physical Education

Year 2 children should be familiar with the routine for PE (changing, and going to the hall or playground), but you will need to explain and establish your own special requirements (where to put clothes; lining up, and so on). By the end of the year, the children should be getting ready more quickly and independently, and will be able to help others prepare for activity. The majority of children will be keen and eager to please but they will require a consistent, firm, but encouraging and supportive environment in order to use their energies in purposeful and positive ways.

In many schools, PE is timetabled three times a week, often with one of these sessions in the playground. For your class this will usually mean one session for gymnastic-type activities with large apparatus, one session for dance and one for games activities.

It is possible that, sometimes, you could use your timetabled time more flexibly, choosing to continue an activity, for instance dance, on subsequent days while interest is buoyant, but make sure you maintain the balance of the three activities throughout the term/year.

If you only have two timetabled hall times you must choose when in the year you teach each of the activities, although you will often be able to take the children outside at other times for games when the weather permits.

You will also find many opportunities to develop other aspects of children's learning (language, mathematics, personal and social experiences) through their physical activities.

Many aspects of learning to move are similar in each of the areas of activity, so some general expectations are included before focusing on more specific expectations for Key Stage 1.

What should they be able to do?

There will be vast differences in experience, interest, physique, temperament, attitude and effort when the children come into your class. Whatever the experiences they have had outside school, or in their first years of schooling, they will still need some help to move safely with others in a large space, on equipment or with apparatus, although they can now be expected to be more aware and independent than when they were younger.

Many children will be agile and energetic and will be able to manage their bodies to stop the actions they are involved in (some more quickly or with greater control than others). They will enjoy playing 'statue' or tag-type games which will sharpen their listening, response and body management. Make the activities fun and provide plenty of encouragement, whether in dance, gym or games and, by the end of the year, most children will be quick, alert and successful in controlling their bodies. All children, apart from those with specific physical impairments, should be able to walk, run, gallop, hop and jump with increasing control and awareness, and many will have a wider range of actions which they can perform successfully (skipping, rolling sideways). By the end of the year they should be developing their ability to clarify or refine their own actions, (point their toes, make a shape clearer)

when asked to do so, or when working with a partner. Observe how they perform these basic actions and encourage them to run on their toes, use their arms in opposition as they walk or run, and use their arms to help them jump.

Many children will also be able to combine actions, for example run and jump; jump and turn; bunny jump moving sideways.

As the year progresses you will notice that they will be able to sustain energetic activity for longer periods, although this will vary tremendously with each individual. They will also be able to comment on, or describe how they feel after exercise (feel hotter, breathe faster).

Although the sequence of progression through the stages of motor development is similar for most children, they do not progress at the same rate, or at an even rate, and so there will always be a wide range of differences in the ways children in your class achieve various actions/ movements. This is natural as every child is unique. Sometimes, through sheer excitement or the demands of the situation, a child will use inconsistent or less advanced movements but, by the end of Year 2, most children's responses should be more consistent. Many will have established a preference for using one hand or one foot but they should still be encouraged to use both.

Key area: Dance

In this year, children will show increasing awareness of a greater range of body parts and most will be able to isolate different parts either to move, to support the body weight or to lead movement. With practise and encouragement, they will be more able to do this in time with the music or sounds, and be able to respond to variations in speed or strength (for instance, shrug shoulders slowly; punch with elbows strongly). As you would expect, there will be great variations in the ways that they do this, some children being more sensitive and aware of differences than others. Most children will enjoy dancing and will be able to move confidently with increasing co-ordination, but some will still need encouragement to control or clarify their actions.

Children are likely to show an increasing ability to use their imagination when given a clear stimulus or framework (pounce like a cat; start high and turn slowly to the ground). Without some guidelines some children will feel uncertain or insecure and may find it difficult to be creative, while others will use the ideas or focus as a jumping-off point for their imaginations.

Most children will be developing their ability to listen and respond to a variety of music or rhythms, to observe and copy actions of others, or to contribute ideas of their own. They will be showing increasing fluency and body management when performing a variety of travelling, turning and jumping actions, and should be able to make their dance more interesting in response to variations in speed, strength and fluency suggested by various forms of accompaniment.

They will also be able to include other actions like rolling, leaping or slithering as their movement vocabulary increases. Encourage them to side-step and skip, or to make up their own step patterns. Most of them will be able to do this rhythmically and continuously in time to music.

They should be developing their ability to use space thoughtfully and well, choosing interesting and varied pathways, (figure of eight, curving, straight, zigzag). They will have some understanding of direction, size and level and can be expected to be able to choose a different direction in which to move or a different level to start when requested to do so. They will show awareness of contrasts in action, shapes, speed, and many will be able to respond and vary the qualities used and begin to combine them (such as turning and rising slowly/quickly; stepping forwards or backwards strongly and jerkily or smoothly and lightly). Most of your class will be able to pick up movements by watching others and repeat short phrases of movement with varying degrees of accuracy and fluency. The children should be increasingly able to describe their actions to others and begin to explain what they liked or found interesting about the movements of others.

Key area: Gymnastics

Most children will be agile, energetic and adventurous, although some may still need lots of encouragement to participate fully, and others may need reminders to be more cautious and aware of others. Give the children plenty of time to practise their running, jumping, sliding, rolling, crawling and climbing actions and to try them in different situations on the floor and then on different parts of the large apparatus.

The children will be able to use a variety of jumping and stepping patterns in their travelling. Encourage them to practise, combine and vary these in the floorwork part of the lesson. Most will be able to hop strongly and rhythmically, but encourage them to use the non-dominant foot as often as possible, and to vary the position of the free leg (stretched out behind/to the side/in front, or knee tucked up to chest/behind). They should be able to hold still, clear shapes (wide, thin , tucked, twisted) on large and small parts of their bodies (sides, tummy, shoulders, seat, one foot or head, hand and foot).

Provide opportunities in every lesson for the children to take their weight on their hands. With their hands flat on the floor and arms straight, as they hold still shapes or move on their hands and feet, they will begin to develop strength in their upper bodies, and be able to move forwards and sideways, for example while bunny jumping or walking on all fours. They will also use their hands to hold on to, climb, hang and pull themselves along on the apparatus.

Most children will be able to share the space and use many parts of the large apparatus confidently. Gradually encourage them to clarify their actions – wider shape; feet together – depending on the focus of the lesson, and help them to develop a greater awareness of what they are doing (such as using the space considerately; landing with better control; slowing down an action) by answering the movement tasks set. They will be developing an awareness of the ways that they can improve their own performance and will be able to link two or more actions into a short sequence.

Key area: Games

Most children at the start of the year will be able to find spaces and use the play area, showing some awareness of others, but they will still need reminders, particularly when concentrating on using equipment. They will be able to play alongside each other showing much more understanding of other children moving but will need help to establish fair turns when sharing apparatus.

The children should take responsibility for looking after the equipment and returning it to the baskets. They should be able to select from a range of equipment when asked to do so and follow instructions.

They will be able to release and guide (roll, tap, throw, kick) a ball with increasing accuracy towards a still target, such as between skittles, into a hoop, to a partner, or between markings on the floor or wall, and many will be able to do this towards a slowly-moving target, such as their partners or a rolling hoop. Whether they are given a target, or choose and make up their own, encourage them to make it more challenging (smaller, further away, narrower). They should be able to stop a ball, control it and take time to take aim at a target, with their feet and with their hands. By the end of the

year, all children should be able to catch a large ball or beanbag thrown up a little way by themselves, relying increasingly just on their hands, and some will be able to do this with a small ball and with a partner. The majority will also be able to bounce and catch a ball (large, medium or small) with two hands (many with one hand) while moving slowly, and count the number of times they can do so. Many children will enjoy using a bat, or their hands, to tap along the ground, tap up or bounce a ball with increasing success. Provide opportunities for them to co-operate and work together in pairs, threes or fours, to share equipment, take turns and make up their own games. As they do so, they will show an increasing ability to negotiate, plan and discuss ideas with others.

Practical ideas

 ## Making a start

Dance

Try different ways for the children to begin their dance lessons. For instance:

▷ clapping, bouncing or moving on the spot to different rhythms (link with music requirements);

▷ moving, shaking, stretching different parts of their bodies (raising awareness of the diferent ways this can be done);

▷ developing and practising travelling actions (marching, creeping, stamping, tip-toeing, striding) with various forms of accompaniment (percussion, music or voice);

▷ using phrases of 16 or 8 beats, this will help your class to use the space, try different variations, respond to the rhythm and gradually raise the heart beat. Children will enjoy doing this to popular tunes or disco music.

Gymnastics

Help children to think about their actions by selecting a focus or theme. They should try out ideas in the floorwork part of the lesson and then on the apparatus. Whatever the theme, you should teach them to handle and use the apparatus carefully, emphasising safety.

Organisation of apparatus

● Divide the class into five or six groups.

● Each group should be responsible for handling the same apparatus each lesson. (Change over each term).

● Make a plan of the apparatus to be used which will support the theme, (for instance, more flat and separate surfaces for balancing).

● Establish a fair and logical pattern of rotation of groups (zigzag, clockwise or, if there are groups with similar apparatus, straight swap) so that, over a period of several lessons, the children can explore fully each group of apparatus in turn. (Set a maximum of, say, two apparatus changes in one lesson.)

● Teach each group how to get out their apparatus (spaced out around apparatus, bending knees not back, holding on, all looking in direction of carrying apparatus) and where to put it. (Use chalk marks initially to help indicate positioning of apparatus).

● Check apparatus fixings and placement before it is used.

● Establish 'ground rules' (for instance, looking where they are going, keeping in a space, not getting too close to others).

● Insist on a quiet working atmosphere and discuss with the children why this is necessary.

● Encourage and help children to share space and equipment (for instance, using the floor space around the apparatus) particularly when there is limited apparatus.

● Establish a consistent routine for stopping, coming down and sitting away from the apparatus.

Sliding and jumping

Focus on specific travelling actions.

▷ **Sliding** – keeping in continuous contact with the floor or apparatus using hands and feet and body parts.

▷ **Jumping with feet** – practise landing safely and carefully before including jumping off benches, planks or trestle tables; try variations – two feet to two feet, one foot to two feet.

▷ **Jumping with hands and feet** (bunny jump). Make sure that hands are flat on the floor with, fingers forward and arms straight and children are in spaces before they bounce their legs and lift them off the floor.

Physical education

Curling and stretching

This will help your class to think about the shape of the body while balancing and moving. Include a combination of moving and still positions in each lesson.

Games

● Use a variety of travelling actions, for instance walk, jog, run, hop, jump, gallop, skip, or stride, to practise stopping, starting, and changing direction. Start on the spot or moving slowly and gradually increase the speed of the action to raise the pulse.

● Some opportunities for free play at the beginning or end of a lesson will allow children to choose pieces of equipment to practise with, working at their own level. This will give you time to observe their needs. It is helpful if you also select and specifically challenge the children to try different actions to increase their movement vocabulary. *Use the other hand/foot. Clap your hands before you catch the ball.*

● Children will be familiar with a variety of equipment, but they will still need your guidance in practising different ways of manipulating and using the equipment. Select from rolling, stopping, collecting, aiming, catching, throwing, kicking, passing, or give a choice of activity with specified apparatus (hoop, rope, ball, quoit).

Introduce individual challenges: *How many? Can you beat your own record?*

● Establish safe and careful use of equipment by encouraging the children to take responsibility for taking it out and putting it away. Explain that they should check that all apparatus has been neatly returned to the baskets, is colour coded and counted. When they are playing in pairs, check that spare equipment has been returned to the baskets.

Developing key areas

Dance

Use a range of rhythmic, body awareness and travelling actions to different forms of accompaniment to begin the lessons. Make it fun by changing the tempo (getting slightly faster or slower) or the strength (lightly, quietly, or strongly) which will develop both their dancing and listening skills. You could use music for marching, like *March Militaire*; music for skipping, like the *Blue Peter* theme, and so on. Percussion can provide a clear stimulus for action, and various rhythms can be explored without the complication of a melody.

Travelling actions and levels

● Repeat travelling actions in short phrases with percussion or simple music accompaniment, for instance walking, tip-toeing, marching, stamping, striding, skipping, slow stepping.

● Work on levels (high, medium, low) and encourage different directions (forwards, sideways, backwards, up and down) and pathways (straight, curving, roundabout, zigzag).

Action words

● Explore the essential qualities in a variety of action words: *wriggle, stamp, bounce, float, collapse.* Choose words with clear contrasts to emphasise particular qualities or aspects of movement (*soar and slither; toss and roll*).With encouragement and practise, children will refine their actions through the use of words, and begin to understand words through their actions, enhancing both their language and dance experiences.

● Words can be used as an accompaniment. It is helpful if they are said in ways which emphasise the actions, *crumple, shake, smooth*, and in phrases to allow the children time to respond. Gradually build a phrase of movement (for example, *toss, toss, toss and flop... creep, creep, creep and creep away*). Encourage children to do this individually and to vary the level at which they are moving or to choose their own starting position.

● Develop both word and action vocabulary by exploring the five basic actions and developing specific qualities (fast/slow, strong/light):
❱ travelling with contrasting speeds – *dodge, rush, stride; sprawl, glide, drift*; or contrasting pathways – *stagger, march, wriggle, slide*;
❱ jumping – *leap, toss, fly, pounce*;
❱ gesturing – *shiver, spread, shrink, melt, twist*;
❱ stopping words – *flop, halt, pause*;
❱ turning – *whirl, spin*.

Stories, topics and objects
● Telling stories through movement captures children's imagination and inspires their interest (for instance, Landing on the moon, Journey through the Jungle).

● Select from relevant stories, or from made-up stories, actions which can be enhanced and developed. For example, under the heading of 'Sea creatures' you might have the sections: Fish; darting, diving, turning. Crabs; scuttling sideways, hiding, opening, closing. Anemone; stretching, waving, closing. Highlight the appropriate qualities as you help the children to explore and practise the actions (dart-dart-dart and turn; dart-dart-dart and pause).

● Use characters or ideas from your topic, for instance Jack Frost, and emphasise the important qualities (spiky, jerky, light, scattering frost high and low, making patterns in the air and on the ground).

● Bring in an object. This can provide a focus of attention which can give security and confidence and provide both a rich source of language and stimulation for movement. For example, if you brought in a stringed puppet the class could discuss its jerky movements (like Pinnochio), and how parts of the body can move individually,

either just one side or the whole body – jumping, turning and collapsing.

Encourage relaxation and a cool down by using slow, swaying music, music for slow walking, or simply calm music which the children can sit or lie and listen to at the end of every lesson.

Gymnastics
Travelling actions
● Develop travelling actions: going towards, away from, around and on the apparatus in straight lines or zigzag pathways, using hands and feet and body parts.

● Encourage the children to select movements which are appropriate to the task set. This will give them a sense of achievement and purpose. Ask them to remember and repeat specific actions and to plan their pathway on the apparatus. This will give them the opportunity to repeat two or three actions one after the other and to practise different ways of linking the actions.

Balancing
● Balancing can be developed by focusing on the number of parts of the body which are taking the weight (touching the floor): four parts (hands and feet; head, hand and feet); three parts (hand and feet; back and feet); two parts (one knee and one hand; both shoulders); one part (back; foot). Encourage the children to hold the shape still for the count of three before moving to a

new space and trying another still shape. In this way they will be moving in their own time and in control of their actions.

● Balancing and linking actions. Build a phrase of action (balance, travel, travel, balance) using hands and feet and body parts. Focus on moving smoothly (lowering down) from the balance into the next action (side roll).

Improving movements

Suggest ways the children can try to make their actions better, such as squashy landings, clearer shape, still balance, and encourage them to talk about ways in which they can improve their own movements or say what they liked about the actions of others.

Children will still need encouragement to use the space well, particularly on the apparatus, where there will often be favourite pieces. Groups will help to ensure fair shares of time using each piece of apparatus.

Games
Class games

Use a variety of class games through the year to start and/or finish the lesson. Start with those with which some children are familiar, like 'Statues' or 'Traffic Lights', and gradually introduce new ones like 'Chase and Change' (A chases B until you shout 'Change', then B chases A. If B is touched before 'Change' is shouted, then B becomes chaser.) In 'Tag' games a few children with bands are the chasers. If touched by a chaser, children stand still with arms outstretched, or legs astride until they are released by one of the other players running under both arms (or between their legs). After a fixed time, the chasers are changed. If everyone is touched before the time is up, new chasers take over.

Games like these encourage listening and quick responses to your stop and start commands. They give opportunities for the children to become more aware of the space and others as they change direction, chase, dodge and weave in and out of each other.

Running and jumping

Encourage different ways of combining running and jumping (for instance over lines, shapes, beanbags or ropes on the floor; hopscotch, and

so on) although some children may find it difficult to concentrate on more than one thing at once, and may initially have problems co-ordinating their actions with the timing.

Ball skills

● When the children have had opportunities to practise individually, encourage them to share and play co-operatively in pairs. This provides a setting for them to help and observe others.

● Travelling and bouncing (dribbling) individually and with a partner: on the spot, walking, changing direction and level, making a pattern of bounces.

● Encourage different ways of throwing and rolling: with two hands/with one hand/ underarm/overarm. Try different positions: sideways/facing/kneeling/standing.

● Catching and throwing individually and with a partner – stationary, moving slowly; close together, further apart.

● Using hand(s) as bat or using medium bat (padder tennis bat) for rolling, stopping, striking and aiming.

Challenges and made-up games

● Most children of this age-group like to test and challenge themselves, so encourage them to beat their own records or to make the action a bit more difficult (a bit higher, a little further away, with the other hand). Suggest they try individually and with a partner.

● Provide opportunities for made-up games in pairs using a specified or chosen piece of equipment. For example, *Make a pattern of bounces with your ball* (two hands, one hand, two hands, or two high bounces, two low bounces, or beat your record) or specify an action (rolling stopping or bouncing). This allows children to be inventive, to use their initiative and to share ideas. They start to become aware of the fundamentals of games played in a situation where they are in control. Challenges such as these introduce simple competitive games. Each child is encouraged to try harder and make the action more difficult without the disappointment of not getting the highest score.

Ideas bank

Dance

● Develop partner work by encouraging pairs to become more sensitive to their partners' actions, adapting their movements to produce a dance together (follow my leader activities – actions, pathways, shapes).

● The more you observe the children's responses, the more ways of developing the creative, expressive forms of dance you will find. Praise interesting ideas and ask children to think of ways of making part of the action clearer. Encourage them to exaggerate the actions and to use their whole body in the movement when it is appropriate.

● Provide lots of contrasting actions (leap and sprawl) and qualities (smoothly or jerkily) which will heighten the experiences for the children and help them recognise and really feel the differences.

Gymnastics

Ask children to:

▶ choose favourite ways of moving (for instance on all fours, on their sides, stretched shapes) and to repeat them, trying ways to make them better;

▶ try specific types of movements (wide shape on hands and feet; travelling on backs or tummies with feet together) to encourage them to think about which actions are appropriate;

▶ practise combining specified actions of their own choice, such as a jump, a balance and a movement on hands, to make an action phrase of linked movements on the floor and on the apparatus.

Games

Provide opportunities to experience running, jumping and throwing in a variety of contexts. Include a variety of running and walking patterns such as long and short strides; giant strides, pigeon steps... fast and slow... accelerating... slowing down... in different directions... in straight lines... curving pathways, zigzag, figure of eight... to a rhythmic beat... around and between obstacles (bean bags, hoops, ropes)... short bursts of speed (following partner, whistle)... and different chasing, catching, seeking, racing games.

Give opportuntities to experience a variety of jumping patterns, over small obstacles (bean bags, or lines on the floor)... from standing... continuously moving... for distance... for height... using both feet or one foot... making patterns of hops, steps and jumps... stepping stones... widening river... hopscotch.

Assessment

Because of the fleeting nature of physical actions, detailed observation is difficult. However, to get a general impression or overall feel for the class response before looking more specifically at the movement of individual children, ask yourself questions such as:

- How do the children respond, listen to my instructions/suggestions?
- How well do they think for themselves/follow others/do a bit of both?
- How well do they use the space? Think how they could be encouraged to use it better.
- Are they able to use different directions? Are they aware of others when they do so? What could I say that might help them?
- How well do they sustain energetic activity? Do I need to make other observations?

Review the class continually, focusing on a few children at a time. Note significant achievement in a child or the class, or look for specific actions or responses.

- Do they use the whole of the body when required?
- Which parts could they make more use of? How controlled are their movements?
- In which ways could they refine their movements? (For instance the fluency of the action.)
- Can they notice, talk about and discuss their ideas and actions in PE?

Dance

- How well do they respond to my voice, the rhythm, sounds or music?
- How imaginative/creative are they?
- Are they achieving the qualities required? When? If not, why not? What might help?
- How well can they isolate and use individual body parts?
- Do they use some parts more fully than others? Do they use different levels on their own volition?
- How well do they remember a phrase or sequence of movements?
- Can they choose their own starting positions from options suggested?
- Can they follow a partner's pathway or match their actions?

Gymnastics

- How well do they use the apparatus? Are there pieces of apparatus which I need to encourage them to use? How inventive are their actions?
- Can they hold still shapes on large and small parts of their bodies for the count of three?
- How confidently can they take their weight on their hands (on all fours, bunny jumps)?
- Can they choose, repeat and refine their favourite movements and select appropriate actions? Can they remember two or three actions and perform them one after the other with a starting and finishing position?

Games

- How well do they move about the space in different directions and in different ways?
- Can they stop, start and weave in and out of each other?
- Can they use the equipment imaginatively and confidently in a variety of ways?
- How accurately can they roll or throw towards a stationary target?

Information and Communication Technology

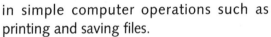

Much of the ICT work you do with Year 2 children will be enhancing the skills they have been developing over the previous few years. They will, by now, be familiar with the three main input devices – keyboard, overlay keyboard and mouse – and most will be confident in simple computer operations such as printing and saving files.

An overlay keyboard (such as the concept keyboard) allows you to customise the input device, so that instead of pressing individual letters, sections of the keyboard can be designated as whole words or even as a drawing. When these are pressed, the appropriate word will appear on the screen. Many children at this age will now be confident in using an overlay keyboard and should be encouraged to use an ordinary keyboard for most work during this year.

To use the mouse effectively requires considerable skill and practise. Over the last few years children should have developed basic mouse skills. Slow down the movement of the mouse for those who are still having difficulties.

What should they be able to do?

At Year 2, children should be familiar with the ways in which information can be put into a computer. They should be aware that computers (or at least microelectronics – the heart of a computer) are to be found in many appliances around their home and at school. During their time in Year 2 they should be taught more about finding and entering information into a computer from a variety of sources, such as CD-ROMs, databases and the Internet using an ordinary keyboard, an overlay keyboard and a mouse. They should be aware of the *enter, backspace, delete* and *shift* keys. They should be able to write simple sentences and to edit their text as they go along and to consider how it can be presented and the information enhanced. They should also have experienced the use of a database for inputting information and presenting it in a graphical way. They should be able to save and print their work. They should be able to use a brush, spray can, fill colours and shapes in graphics programs. Finally, they should be familiar with a simple floor robot, be aware that it can be controlled remotely and be able to extend this knowledge to the use of Logo on a computer screen.

Practical ideas

Making a start

Editing text

Provide the children with a short story or nursery rhyme both on paper and as a word-processor file. The computer file version should have a number of mistakes in it which the children should correct using the paper version as a reference. This is an ideal opportunity to develop children's use of the cursor keys to move around the text (up, down, left and right) as well as using the mouse, and to teach children how to use the *Del* (delete) and *Bksp* (backspace) keys. (*Del* for removing the character in front of the flashing cursor and *Bksp* for removing the character behind the cursor).

Producing name labels

Ask the children to write their name using a word-processing program. They should then:

 ▶ enlarge the text size to 36pt (and change the font if they wish);

 ▶ centre the text on the page;

 ▶ use a rectangle tool to draw a border around the name;

 ▶ select an interesting line style;

 ▶ choose a clipart picture and insert it at one corner of the name label;

 ▶ save the file and print it out.

This activity can be done with the assistance of your more computer-literate pupils. Teach them to act as peer tutors, assisting and supporting the other children in the class, but not doing the task themselves. (Be aware, though, that not all children have the patience to do this.)

Computers at home

As homework, ask children to make a list of all the things at home which they think are like computers or have parts of computers within them. Collate all the ideas during a class discussion and make a list of all the items that have some microelectronics in them. With the children decide upon the main features of electronic devices. For instance, many of them will have digital displays – microwaves, VCRs, alarm clocks, and so on.

Developing key areas

Using CD-ROMs for research

Children should be able to start to search for information on CD-ROMs, but the task must be well-structured if any worthwhile learning is to take place. It is very easy for a child to find information on a particular topic, but often the information is at too sophisticated a reading level, and in many cases inappropriate. Give the children some very clear questions which you want answered, and make sure that the answers are, in fact, available using the CD-ROM. *My First Incredible Amazing Dictionary* is a very suitable CD-ROM for this age-group.

Work of artists

Choose an artist and have a wide selection of his/her paintings available in the form of posters, postcards and books. Discuss with the children the main characteristics of the artist's work. The use of colour, the texture of the work, the way in which people are painted and the content of the pictures themselves. When you have created a list of the important features, ask the children to produce a painting of their own using a paint program which has similar characteristics. With this age-group, this activity will obviously be carried out at a very simple level, but it will allow children to identify particular features of artists' work and to make full use of the tools that are available on Paint programs including brush tools of various widths and spray can tools.

Household appliances

Building on the discussion of items in the home which have microelectronics included in them, ask pairs of children to produce their own database of household appliances. Many children will need support in the form of an outline database, but some may be able to make an attempt at devising one of their own. The sort of questions you would want answered would be: *Which devices are the most common in the home? Which devices are controlled electronically?* and *Which devices need electricity in order to work?*

Exploring tessellations

Use a program which can put together tiles of different shapes and colours to produce tessellated patterns. *My World* with the *Tiles* package is an ideal example of this, although there are many others. Start simply by getting the children to tessellate square tiles. Then allow them to experiment with more intricate shapes and colours. Show them how they can flip the tiles both vertically and horizontally.

Screen Logo

Remind children of the work they will have done with floor robots. Introduce them to a screen-based control program such as *Baby Logo*. Here they use the same ideas of *Forward, Backwards, Right Turn* and *Left Turn,* but instead of a robot moving around the floor, a turtle shaped object moves around the screen, leaving a trail. This means that the program can actually be used to draw shapes. At this stage, the children should concentrate on drawing squares and rectangles. This helps to reinforce maths work on the properties of 2-D shapes (in a square all the sides are the same length; in a rectangle opposite sides are the same length). Work on Logo will be developed further in later years.

Parts of a plant

After having discussed the parts of a plant, ask children to draw their own picture of a plant and to label each part using a paint program. For children who need extra support, provide a basic outline of the plant, which they can enhance and label themselves. This idea can be adapted for various uses, for example, naming parts of the body.

Travelling down a ramp

Ask the children to bring in a toy vehicle from home (or use school ones). They must have moving wheels. Ask the children to name their vehicles. Each child then puts the vehicle at the top of a ramp and it is then timed to see how long it takes to get to a fixed point on the floor. The child types the vehicle's name and the time it took to travel down the ramp (in seconds) into a spreadsheet you have already prepared. When all the class have entered their information, display a barchart to show the quickest and the slowest vehicles. Discuss the shape of the bar chart. As extension work you could develop the format of the spreadsheet so that each vehicle can have three turns. It is the average of the three times which would be shown on the bar chart. This activity ties in with work on forces in science.

Ideas bank

My calendar

This activity demonstrates the power of modern computer programs to produce high quality results. A desktop publishing program, such as *Microsoft Publisher* has a number of 'wizards' which automatically produce layouts to a high standard. By selecting the 'calendar wizard' it is possible to produce automatically an A4 calendar for any year, by making a very limited number of choices to the layout. If children have produced designs using a paint package these could be incorporated into the calendar design. Print the calendars on card (or print on paper and stick on to card) to make very good Christmas presents for the children to take home. If you do not have a colour printer, the design can be coloured in on the black and white print.

Making a T-shirt

Ask the children to produce a picture using a paint package which illustrates something in which they are interested. They should incorporate their name somewhere into the design. Print this on special paper using an ordinary black and white or colour ink-jet printer. The design can then be ironed onto a plain T-shirt (the children can watch, but this part must be done by adults). This provides very good motivation for them to develop their computer drawing skills and, if you use new T-shirts and sell them to the children, it is a good fund-raiser for the school. If you know that parents cannot afford to buy new T-shirts, ask if the children can bring a T-shirt in from home to be decorated.

Making a postcard

The children can combine text and graphics (either a drawing of their own, or some clip-art) to produce a postcard which they could send to one of their friends or relations. Print the work out on paper and then stick it onto card for posting. (Combine this with writing activities in English.) The same technique can be used to produce cards for birthdays, Christmas, Mother's day, Eid, Easter, Diwali, and so on.

Assessment

By the end of Year 2 you would expect children to be able to:

● use Information and Communication Technology as part of their work in a number of curriculum areas;

● retrieve information from a CD-ROM and the Internet;

● produce word-processed text using a keyboard;

● correct mistakes by using the *cursor* and *Del* (delete) and *Bksp* (back space) keys;

● print work out using the *print* command;

● input data into a simple database;

● interrogate a database to find the answers to simple questions;

● produce some artwork using an art package, making use of the mouse;

● paint pictures with straight lines and appropriate regular shapes, saving and loading between sessions;

● make a screen robot trace out simple regular shapes.

Information and communication technology

Design and Technology

In Year 2, designing and making should be practised in a variety of contexts and with a range of materials. The aim is to develop design and technology capability as a combination of know-how and know-what. The National Curriculum specifies some areas of knowledge, skills and understanding but design and technology draws on others, such as concepts from science and mathematics.

Some design and technology activities in Year 2 develop knowledge and understanding. For instance, an everyday object or toy might illustrate some mechanism. It might be examined, mentally disassembled, parts named and explained. Another activity might be to develop and practise a skill or way of doing something. A focused practical task often serves this purpose. The task may be used to develop either a designing skill such as elaborating an idea, or a making skill such as sawing strip wood to length. By themselves, these tasks are unlikely to provide sufficient opportunities for Year 2 children to develop and show their designing and making capabilities. A simple, practical problem which requires some independent designing and making is better suited to this. In Year 2, you may limit the choice of materials to those that are likely to be useful and hence provide clues to ensure a successful start.

Progression in Year 2

It is important that there is the opportunity for progression in design and technology capability. In Year 2, contexts are wider and technological knowledge is extended to include, for instance, some pneumatics and simple electrical control. Materials may require more shaping than in earlier years because you will not have pre-prepared them to the same extent. You introduce variations in joining and fastening and expect a higher quality of finish (for example, children paint to, cut along and fix on a line). At the same time, your support is likely to be less immediate. Children of different capabilities can often attempt the same task. In essence, this is differentiation by outcome. Tune a task to particular children's capabilities by the amount of support you provide and the reserve you show in intervening. The same problem may also be set with different degrees of openness, for example, *We need something to stop the door slamming* and *We need a door stop*. One can be easier than another.

Year 2 children should be developing some skill in using simple hand tools but they may lack some fine motor skills and act thoughtlessly on occasions. Safety is paramount. Remember to consider the safety of the child using the tool, the safety of others and also of yourself. The place where the children use the tools should be in view. Store tools securely and check them regularly. Repair or replace immediately any that could be unsafe. Expect Year 2 children to take some responsibility for safe practices and for keeping their workspace clear and tidy.

What should they be able to do?

When they begin Year 2, children should already have experienced making things by following their teacher's instructions. They will also have had some opportunities to practise simple aspects of designing.

This is built upon in Year 2 by:

- extending their awareness of the manufactured world;
- developing their awareness of what counts in design & technology capability;
- increasing the variety of contexts;
- developing and extending designing skills;
- extending making skills;
- increasing technological knowledge and understanding.

Key area: Contexts

Design and technology activities drawn from your broader topics can help to integrate the curriculum but you may want to do a separate topic for design and technology on some occasions. In Year 2, such contexts and activities will tend to relate to the home, the school and the immediate environment. By using theses locations the children will be able to see their relevance.

Key area: Planning and making skills

Inadequate designing often leads to failure in making. For instance, children are often vague about 'special' bits, like how to attach an axle. There is no formula to follow but they should practise generating and clarifying ideas and choosing what is likely to succeed. Several ways of communicating ideas need to be practised, such as verbally, freehand drawings with some labels, simple models, and so on. You will have to teach some technological knowledge and know-how directly, for instance, what could be used to keep a wheel in place.

There may be instances when children design one thing and make another. When they are making, their drawings should be in front of them to act as reminders. However, they should be aware that they may have to modify their designs as they proceed in order to meet unanticipated difficulties. Avoid responding too quickly in such situations. Ask the child for suggestions first.

By the end of Year 2, the majority of children should:

- know which tools to use for working a range of common materials, like paper, card, thin plastic sheet, wood strip, clay, food, textiles;
- be able to practise, measure (eg by comparison) and mark out what they need, avoiding waste;
- be able to make practical suggestions about what to do next and consider other ways of proceeding;
- know how to join and combine a range of common materials and components and be able to choose, justify and apply some finishes (eg paint, fabric, PVA to give a gloss finish, pictures and patterned paper).
- Use finishing techniques to improve their work.
- Follow safe working procedures and be aware of food safety and hygiene.

Key area: Knowledge and understanding of materials and components

Since materials appropriate to a task should be used, choose contexts carefully to avoid introducing more than one new material at a time. Sometimes only familiar materials should be used to consolidate working skills. A wide range of materials is possible (paper, card, plastics, wood, metal foils) but supply them in forms which can readily be manipulated by Year 2 children (for instance, 1 cm square section wood strip, 1 mm thick plastic sheet). Components at this stage include the parts of kits, simple switches, wires and light bulbs. In Year 2, children need to add knowledge of how levers work to their repertoire of mechanisms. Energy to make things move will often be provided by the children themselves or gravity. They should use a switch in a circuit with a torch bulb and compare it with switches in electrical toys.

Structures: The children should learn about how objects (such as traffic cones) are made stable by giving them a wide base, how they are strengthened by using stiffeners (like the triangular pieces of wood attached to the underside of some chair seats), and how certain shapes have more strength than others (like tubular table legs or L-shaped angle iron).

Products and applications: Children should investigate how products have been made, assembled and finished to make them suitable for their purpose. Toys, common classroom objects and safe household items are often suitable for this purpose. At this stage, they might compare several different versions of a product and evaluate them.

Quality: Encourage children to be concerned about the quality of the product (for example, removing excess glue). Is it well-made for its purpose?

Health and safety: Continue to teach children to avoid injury to themselves and others. They could make a safety poster for the design and technology workplace, explaining how to use a tool safely, stating dangers, and so on.

Vocabulary: Appropriate vocabulary for what they use and do should be extended (axle, stiffener, lever arm, pivot, tube).

Working at higher or lower levels

Sometimes, working at other levels is achieved by altering the degree of support you provide. It is possible to provide simpler tasks with different contexts, but this can make a child's inadequacies, real or otherwise, apparent. An alternative is to use a context which allows a variety of possible products (such as a fairground) or materials (for instance, puppets). Allocate tasks so that all are working at an appropriate level, consolidating and developing skills. If you have a child with special needs, this approach can be a sensitive solution.

Challenge children with well-developed design and technology capability by withholding some support, by expecting more know-how in their products, and by providing extension tasks which develop their product beyond the original brief. A castle drawbridge, for instance, can be raised in different ways. A simple solution is to use a drawstring. One requiring more know-how is to use some kind of winder which takes up the string and raises the bridge.

Practical ideas

 ## Making a start

You can use the ideas described below directly, adapt them or use them as models for activities within the topics you use.

You may be working on a broad topic such as houses and homes or you may focus on a particular area of the curriculum such as science (electricity) or history (castles). These can generate design and technology work on, for instance, structures (houses) and mechanisms (the drawbridge). A recent event in school, a picture which suggests a problem, a story or a visit which sets the scene for a problem can capture the children's interest. Teach them to clarify their design ideas by responding to *What? Why? How?* questions and by explaining and justifying their intentions. While making, they should be aware of what is and is not working well. They need to learn that changing the shape of materials, for example by folding, can change their properties, and that materials can be joined in a number of ways.

 ## Developing key areas

Contexts

Children need to see purpose and interest in what they do. Elicit knowledge and know-how and relate this to the task in hand. Some strategies follow.

Stories

Use stories which lead up to a need or problem which is then resolved. Stop at the point where the need or problem has emerged and discuss how the situation might be resolved. The children design and make to satisfy the need. Then return to the story and show them how it was resolved. For example, in *The Mice and the Clockwork Bus* by Rodney Peppe (Viking Kestrel, 1986), Mr Rat takes the mice to school in his somewhat dangerous 'bus'. After it crashes, the mice decide to build a new bus from reclaimed materials. The

children can discuss possibilities, draw one and make it. The story is then resumed, showing the children what the mice do.

Visits

Visits which relate to other areas of the curriculum can have a design and technology element. For instance, a visit to High Street shops could be followed by making a meal.

Challenges

In a sense, all design and technology tasks are challenges but it refers here to when a task is presented explicitly in that form. *Let's see who can make a buggy which will run down this hill and go from here to that wall.*

Visitors

You may be able to find a local workshop or small factory where things which interest children are made. For instance, there may be a toymaker who is willing to visit the school and make some simple toys in front of the children, or if there is a local factory which produces stuffed toys they may be able to send a visitor or let you borrow one of the toys in its different stages of production. These can serve as starting points, leading to children designing and making simple toys, such as buggies or puppets.

Designing
Exploring the task

You will need to ensure that the children understand what the task means and what it encompasses. Ask questions to stimulate the recall of relevant prior knowledge and to check on vocabulary. *Let's see who can tell the rest of us what we are going to do. What do we already know about...? What ideas do you have? What materials have we used before to make...?* Supplement this knowledge so that the task is meaningful and, if possible, use situations that are local to your environment. For example, if there are road works near the school, children could design and make a warning light for the hole in the road.

Design and technology (side margin)

Stimulating ideas and focusing

To help children generate ideas, state the problem and accept the responses to it. Review them in turn and have the children consider what is feasible in the classroom and what has most chance of success. *I don't have any rope. What might we use instead?* Do not forget to be explicit about 'special' bits. *How can we make sure the axles will be the same length?*

Developing new knowledge

Develop additional knowledge by using everyday objects. Ask the children to examine them and explain how they work. Some things, such as a press-top ball-point pen, might safely be dismantled and re-assembled. Pictures can be used in the absence of the real thing.

Making
Choosing materials

The children will have considered materials at the designing stage but now they may be faced with variations. Materials come in a variety of forms and sizes. Expect children to do some simple marking out, for example they might draw around a template on felt and cut to the line. Stress the importance of using materials conscientiously to avoid waste.

Modelling

Young children are sometimes so eager to make something that they fix things together and then find that things do not fit, can no longer be fitted, are upside down, and other faults which, as adults, we tend to see as thoughtless. The aim is to develop the habit of trying things loosely before fixing permanently. Encourage the children to assemble the components and to make sure they are the correct way around. Have them check they can still fit the final items. A common mistake, for instance, is for children to put wheels on axles before they put the axles through the axle support holes.

Quality

The purpose of the exercise is not simply to make a product which works or satisfies a need. By now, you should be able to draw attention to matters of appearance, cutting along a line, fixing pieces together so their edges line up, and the need for their products to be reliable.

Introducing new ideas

Contexts

In each of these examples, an introduction is provided, a related practical task is given and further development is suggested. They may be used as they are, adapted, or may serve as models for other activities.

Paper and card: moving pictures

Show the children books with pictures which move, especially those that pop up when a lever is moved or a disc is turned.

Show a very simple card with a moving part which uses a lever. Disassemble it and show how it works. Have the children make a version of it.

Suggest an occasion when a greetings or celebration card would be appropriate (for example, a birthday, Valentine's Day, Mother's Day, Easter) and help the children develop ideas which include a moving part. They then make the card.

Fabrics: the theatre

The children watch a puppet show on television or video. Afterwards, tell them a short story which has two characters in it and discuss what the puppets for this story might be like.

Show the children a simple puppet (for example, a finger puppet or one made from card using paper-fasteners). Disassemble it and show how it is made. The children then make a similar figure for the story.

Ask the children to make another figure to represent the other character and act out the story with the puppets.

Wood: animals

Read a story which involves a wriggling animal (for instance *The Very Hungry Caterpillar*, Eric Carle). Display some simple, wooden toy animals of this kind and discuss them with the class.

Show the children a snake made from short pieces of wood fixed together with fabric to allow movement. Using strip wood, demonstrate how to saw it into short lengths. Show how it can be glued to a strip of fabric to make a floppy snake. (The wood could be painted in a snake pattern before it is sawn.) Cut out a tongue from felt and glue it on. The children can then practise sawing by making snakes. They could make a three-dimensional jungle background to provide an environment for their snakes. (Snakes might also be made with bobbins, held together loosely by string.)

What other animals could we make like this? For example, minibeasts like the bee, ant, and the centipede could fit in with science work. Have the children design and make one. *How could we make some wings for the bee? What could we use for eyes?*

Recycled materials: lights

Following work with simple switches, batteries, wires and bulbs in science, discuss when, where and why we use lights. Show the children a table lamp. Warn them about the dangers of mains electricity.

Together, construct a battery-operated circuit with a light bulb in a holder on a card tube.

The children could go on to make a battery-operated table lamp using recycled materials. The lamp should switch on and off.

Food: bread rolls

Tell a story about a picnic or a party which involves food. Ask the children to list what they think is needed for such an event. Discuss matters of hygiene and ensure the children's hands are clean.

The children disassemble a ready-made sandwich. Look at its contents and make a list with the class. Discuss healthy eating.

The children mix and knead some bread dough. Bake rolls for them and discuss various fillings. Provide some and let them choose and use them. Have the rolls for lunch.

Ideas bank

● As well as cards which use a lever pivoted with a paper-fastener, the children can make cards with rotating discs. These bring information into view through a window cut into a covering card. They can be used to show *Today is....* The day of the week or date is rotated into view, or the weather is shown in symbols.

● Use small boxes as bodies for buggies. Cardboard egg boxes work well and provide hollows for goods or for play people to sit in. Axle action may be introduced by having the children make a top using a wheel and a short length of dowel. Ready-made wheels may prove expensive if every child is to make a buggy, but they do increase the chance of success. Plastic lids from jars, corks and card wheels may be used as an alternative but care will be needed when fixing them on axles.

● Puppets may be made in many ways. At their simplest, they can be made by gathering scraps of fabric into appropriate shapes with rubber bands. Thick string can serve for arms and legs. Fabric finger- and card shadow-puppets are popular. Puppets suspended from strings are easy to make if the children limit themselves to making only the arms move. Stages for these puppets can be made from large cardboard boxes and decorated appropriately.

● Once children have mastered how to make a circuit which operates a light bulb, they can use coloured translucent sweet papers to make different coloured lights for traffic lights or pedestrian crossings. (This could have a road safety context.) Christmas tree lights may also be made. A hand-operated switch will make them flash.

● To develop work on stability, demonstrate how a large bunch of plastic flowers in a tall narrow vase may easily overbalance. This sets the scene for the problem. Make a vase which will not fall over and which looks attractive. Kitchen roll tubes can serve as a vase which needs adapting by, for instance, fixing something to its base to widen it and/or putting something inside to weight it.

● Introduce children to clay work by making something in which to store pencils (perhaps a large ladybird with holes in it) or a small clay figure with a magnet to hold messages on a refrigerator door. Clays which harden without firing are available. Ribbons of magnetic material are easy to cut and stick and are available from most educational suppliers.

● Pneumatics need not involve complex equipment. For instance, children might see the hand (Thing) that comes from a box in an *Addams Family* film and make one themselves using an empty tea-bag box, a plastic glove and a straw to inflate it. Similarly, a Jack or Jill-in-the-Box may be made using a small, plastic sandwich bag which lifts a play person from a small box when inflated through a straw. (See illustrations)

● A story about a zoo could be used to introduce 'Snappy Animals': animal heads made from two flat pieces of wood which are hinged at one end with tape. A piece of ribbon can be stapled between the pieces of wood to look like a tongue. Scraps of wood can serve as eyes and nostrils. Fabric tails and painted teeth may be added. Wood should be of such a shape and size that it does not require extensive sawing to make the required animal. It should also be 'dressed', that is, already be smooth. A number of simple, wooden toys may be made by Year 2 children (a framework for a swing for dolls, a car or boat from blocks of wood that are glued together to give the required shape, a simple table and chairs for a doll's house, and so on). Wood should be held by an appropriate device before cutting (a vice or bench hook, for instance).

● Draw silhouettes around tools in a tray. This allows tools to be easily found and checked. The children should develop the habit of returning the tools to their place immediately after use.

● Old and new. History provides a good context for studying artefacts. Old artefacts can be compared with their recent counterparts (irons and coathangers, for instance). There are toys, which owe their novelty to the use of more-recently-developed materials, for example, high bouncing balls, play 'goo', and Velcro on a hat for catching a fabric ball.

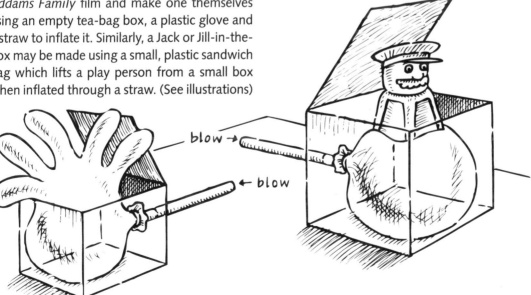

blow →
← blow

Assessment

In design and technology, both knowledge and skills are assessed. While a finished product can provide some evidence of skills, it cannot tell you everything about the child's work. In particular, you need to know about those designing and making skills which are not always visible in the end product. For instance, were the children able to adapt their design as they worked? Did they work safely and tidily? This means that you need to observe them as they work.

What do they know?

The children should know:
● some simple mechanisms, such as wheels and axles, the lever, a simple push-pull device;
● about simple structures, such as tubes, building from bricks, shock-absorbent shapes, stable shapes;
● how some everyday objects function;
● which tools to use to cut and shape the materials they have used;
● the correct vocabulary with which to discuss the tools, materials and technological matters relating to the products they have made and disassembled.

What can they do?

The children should:
● begin to generate some ideas relevant to the task in hand;
● be able to produce a drawing of what they will make and add labels to it;
● begin to make realistic suggestions about how to proceed and accept compromise solutions;
● begin to think ahead about the order in which they will do things so that some difficulties can be avoided;
● choose materials, tools and techniques purposefully;
● use tools with some accuracy, cutting and shaping materials with sufficient precision for assembling the product;
● be able to choose and apply a particular finish;
● produce results which are perceptibly similar to their intentions and should be able to identify any changes.

Religious Education

Religious Education has to be planned from a local rather than a national document. Agreed syllabuses differ in the way they present the programme of study but are similar in what they expect children to do in RE. It is likely that your agreed syllabus expects children to:

- develop a knowledge and understanding of religious traditions;
- explore fundamental questions arising out of people's experience of life;
- develop their own ideas and values arising partly out of what they learn in RE.

In terms of continuity and progression in RE, you should be helping your pupils to acquire a systematic knowledge and understanding of some religions as well as developing their thinking and understanding about religious issues and common themes across religions. This will contribute to their understanding of religion in general.

Religious Education can be approached in various ways, for instance through 'systems' topics and 'human experience' topics. Human experience topics focus on a fundamental question or issue about life, such as *Who is my neighbour?* or *Why are we here?* 'Systems' topics concentrate on an aspect of one particular religion. The example followed through here for Year 2 is a systems topic because its main focus is to teach children something about one religion, in this case Christianity.

In Key Stage 1, emphasis is often placed on the human experience approach. Younger children may well have explored themes such as 'Caring for others' or 'Caring for our World'. In Year 2, children will still need to learn through the human experience approach but it is also important to begin to introduce them to religion through the systems approach. If you do this at the end of Key Stage 1, you are preparing them for Key Stage 2, when they will be exploring some of the basic practices associated with religions. The chosen topic in this chapter, exploring infant baptism, is a focus for beginning to understand something about Christianity.

What should they be able to do?

By the time they reach Year 2, most children are at a stage where they can begin to develop their capabilities for classifying and organising concepts. Their natural curiosity makes it possible to open up for them a world of unfamiliar people, places, events and actions. The topic on baptism begins this process gently. Most children should be able to explore, in a limited way, the relationship between learning about religion and learning from it.

The topic of baptism is about more than merely acquiring information about baptism. It relates the concept of baptism to the human experience concepts of relationship and community. The idea of community is developed by exploring the importance of **church** for Christians. The emphasis on words and actions should enable children to begin to understand the context of such words and actions within the Christian community; for example, 'joining' and 'belonging'. This will help them to think about their own responses to the content of the topic.

Key area: Knowledge and understanding of religions

Children in Year 2 develop their knowledge and understanding of religions largely through contact with people, concrete examples and stories. In this topic, the outward expressions of baptism and church life will provide the focus for their learning. Beliefs and spiritual insights are implied rather than given explicit treatment. Concept development is an essential component of good RE teaching at any level. The range of Christian concepts that could be explored in this topic is wide but the most appropriate one for this age is the concept of **church**. Another useful concept is that of **initiation**. This is a concept derived not from any one particular religion but from the study of religion in general. It is a significant word for children to learn as it will be applicable in a number of contexts later on in their RE lessons.

Teach the children about the order and procedure of the baptism ceremony and certain roles within this ceremony. Through the activities in this topic introduce them to some aspects of the life and role of the church as a worshipping community for Christians.

Another vital aspect of good RE teaching is the raising of important questions. In the context of this element, there are several Christian 'answers' to such questions as *What happens to children when they are baptised?* and *What is baptism for?* Such questions can be answered at different levels and part of your role as a teacher is to help children perceive these different levels. For example, some children may respond at a very basic, descriptive level to a question such as, *What happens to children when they are baptised?* Other, more able children, should be encouraged to look beyond the merely descriptive. It is also part of your job to give children the opportunity to respond personally to such questions. (This is dealt with under the Key area: Responding to religion and human experience.)

Key area: Exploring human experience

Children in Year 2 will be familiar with significant events in their own family life such as birthdays and anniversaries. However, they may not be familiar with specific Christian ceremonies. Encourage them to talk about other examples of 'joining' ceremonies to help them understand the concept of initiation. In this way, also, children can be introduced to the concept of community, which is derived from our shared human experience and is an important dimension of religious life for believers in many religious traditions. An understanding of this concept within the context of Christian baptism will not only help them come to a greater understanding of the Christian tradition, but will also help to equip them with a concept through which to understand other religious practices in their further studies. Raising questions in this area is also good practice, so encourage the children to think about why people, in general, feel the need to become part of communities, why they need to belong and why they feel the need to mark this by celebrating special occasions.

Key area: Responding to religion and human experience

Responding to questions plays an essential role in this element. However, rather than considering specific questions about Christian baptism, or general questions about our shared human experience, children should be given the opportunity to respond personally. A vital aspect of this area is to encourage them in their own responses. Help them to learn how to answer questions with statements like 'I think....' or 'I believe...' This helps them to appreciate that people are allowed to respond to significant questions in their own way which will enable them to begin to adopt positive attitudes, such as respect for others' points of view.

Practical ideas

 ## Making a start

Introducing baptism through artefacts

Obtain a baptism candle, a scallop shell and a bottle of holy water. Wrap each object. Organise the class into a circle and pass each package around. Ask the children to feel it all over and then to pass it on to their neighbour. Tell them to remember what it feels like. When everyone has felt each package, ask the children for descriptions and guesses for each one. Reveal each artefact and ask the children what they might be used for, who might use them and what they might have in common. Answer these questions if children do not give the answers. Display a large-format picture of infant baptism and point out the objects. Explain that these objects show that this baby has joined a big family called a **church**. Discuss what they know about church.

Tell a story

It is always good to introduce religious practices through the life of a child. Use a story such as *Colin's Baptism* (Olivia Bennett, Evans Brothers). Discuss the story and ask children to look for any special baptism objects in the pictures. Children can talk about what they have heard about their own baptism or naming ceremony or that of a baby in the family. Ask if any of the children would be able to bring into class any special objects relating to their baptism or naming that belong to them.

Have a discussion

Discuss examples of groups to which children belong, for example, their families, Beavers, and so on. Talk about joining ceremonies associated with groups and ask any children who belong to such a group to bring into school anything that may be of interest.

Arrange a visit

Arrange for the children to visit a local church and be shown the font. Enquire whether the vicar/priest would be able to meet the children and read some of the words from the baptism service to them – particularly the promises made by the parents and godparents – and answer any questions they may have.

Invite a family

Invite a Christian family, who have recently had their child baptised, to visit the class. Let the children see the infant and ask the mother and/ or father about the service. Ask if the family would be prepared to bring in any clothes or objects connected with the baptism.

Show a video

Show the class a video of an infant baptism and allow the children to talk about what they have seen. Encourage them to use appropriate language such as 'font', 'baptism' 'godparent'.

Introducing new key areas

A topic on baptism is an ideal opportunity to introduce children to the meaning of symbolism in religion. This will have to be done in a very gradual way. The emphasis is best placed on key elements of the baptism ceremony such as naming and the use of water and light.

Talk about names

The naming of a baby is important in all faiths. (For naming customs in other faiths see the Ideas bank on page 158.) Talk to the children about names and how they often have special meanings. Many children have names of Biblical characters or saints, for example Ruth, Rebecca, Naomi, Judith, Elizabeth, Sarah, Rachel, Deborah, Luke, Matthew, Paul, David, Daniel, Timothy. Talk about how these names have been used for many years and how Christian parents may have chosen these names because of their biblical connections.

Let the children talk about their names and what they know about them. Give each child a card containing the words *'My name is...', 'My name means...','I have the same name as...', 'I was called... because...'*. Some of these may have to be taken home for their parents to fill in. (Be sensitive to the fact that some children in your

class may be unable to contribute anything about the history of their names.) When the cards have been filled in, have further discussions with the children about names and the different reasons parents have for choosing them. *When you have children of your own, what will you call them? Why?*

Look at some pictures of fonts

Try and collect a selection of pictures of fonts.(Resource Centres should be able to help you. Refer to the Resources and suppliers section on page 159.) Discuss the differences between the fonts and talk about how they are used. Explain that in all cases water is used.

Discuss uses of water

Make a collection of pictures which show the various uses of water. Concentrate on the different ways water is used for cleansing things or people.

Several activities can be developed from this discussion. For instance, you could ask a parent to come in and demonstrate how their baby is bathed. Have some dolls available for the children to bath or clean. Discuss why we need to bath and wash our hands. Then discuss various washing routines for special occasions like parties. Muslim children may want to talk about the ritual washing before prayer (see Ideas bank).

Read a Bible story

Read the story of the baptism of Jesus by John the Baptist. You will find this in Matthew, chapter 3, verses 13–17. Explain to the children that Christians believe that Jesus is God's son and that this is why baptising with water is so important

for many Christians. Discuss with the children how they feel after a bath or a good wash. *Do you feel clean? Fresh? Brand new?* Explain that, in a very special way, Christians believe that being baptised makes them feel like new.

Read another Bible story

Tell or read the story of Jesus taking small children on his knee (Matthew, chapter 28, verses 18–20). Explain that Christians tell this story to show how God loves all people including very young babies. When they baptise children, they are expressing this belief and welcoming the child into the Christian family. If you have children of other faiths in your class, talk about how their naming ceremonies welcomed them into the Muslim/Hindu/Sikh/Jewish families.

Re-enact a baptism

You can either do this with the help of a vicar or you can do it yourself. It is ideal if you can use the local church and the font. Choose a mother and father, godparents, and so on and use a doll as a baby. Hold a class discussion about possible names for the baby (it could have several) and vote on them. Adapt the words from the baptism service. (You can find the Anglican one in *The Alternative Service Book*, 1980.) Re-enact the service and then discuss with the children how they felt, what they noticed, and so on. Afterwards ask the children to write a short descriptive piece about what they have experienced.

Discuss light as a symbol

Sit the children in a circle and refer back to the first activity 'Introducing baptism through artefacts'. Show the children a baptism candle. Some have decorations on them such as a shell and a dove. Refer back to the ceremony and the Bible story of Jesus' baptism to explain these. Light the candle and ask the children to sit quietly for a moment and to think about what the light means to them. Discuss the answers and then ask the children to write a poem entitled 'Light means...' Alternatively you may prefer to do this as a class poem.

Jesus as 'Light of the World'

Read the short passage from St John's Gospel chapter 8, verse 12. Discuss what the term may mean. Paint a picture to illustrate this.

✦ Developing key areas

This section is designed to develop the children's understanding of the Christian concept of church. It concentrates largely on the church as a building but in your teaching try also to develop the idea of church meaning a group of people who believe in Jesus. If you have children of other faiths in the class, make sure that, when talking about the church, you also bring in references to temples, mosques, gurdwaras and synagogues and encourage them to see the common ground between their faith communities and the Christian community.

Visit a church

Take the children to a local church. If the vicar is used to small children, ask if he or she will show them around and talk to them. Study the architecture and furnishings and discuss what they are used for and what goes on inside a church. The children can talk, write and draw about various aspects of their visit. Make a display of their work.

Look at some pictures

Gather together a collection of different pictures of the outside of churches: country churches, modern churches, cathedrals, and so on. Discuss their differences and shapes. Make a display.

Learn more about the church

A good book that deals in a simple way with belonging to a church is *A First Look at the Church* (Lois Rock, Lion). This deals with worship, celebrations, living as a family, and so on. Explore all these different aspects with the children. Divide the class into groups and give each group a different aspect to study. Ask them to write about their aspect and draw some accompanying pictures. Make a display of their work and give it a title such as 'What we have learned about the Church'.

We found pictures of many different churches

Let the children talk

Encourage children to talk about their experience of church or Sunday school (Include temple, mosque, gurdwara, and so on as appropriate). Ask them to say what they do there and how they feel about being with friends and sharing in activities. (An excellent resource to explore what Sunday means to a Christian child is *Lucy's Sunday*, Bridges to Religions series, Heinemann. The teacher's book contains good ideas and some useful worksheets.)

Use a guided fantasy

Sit the children in a circle and ask them to be quiet while you talk to them about going to a special place. When you have finished, ask them to imagine a place which is special to them to which they go regularly.

Then encourage them to talk about this special place. *How do you feel when you are there? Why is it special to you?* Ask them to draw a picture and write about their special place.

For more help on guided fantasy, the book, *Don't Just Do Something: Sit There* by Mary K Stone (Religious and Moral Education Press) is helpful. It explains how to set up and develop guided fantasy lessons. Material is provided on special places which you could adapt for your own needs.

 ## Ideas bank

This chapter on baptism does not explore RE in a thematic way. However, here are some ideas about how you might develop some of the themes in the topic and apply them to other religious traditions.

Be careful because poor thematic teaching can lack focus and the children may become confused or learn little of importance. Aim to be very clear about what you want to concentrate on and make sure that any links you make between the religions are conceptually clear. Because of this you will not find any ideas about initiation in this section. Baptism as initiation is a particularly Christian thing and you cannot find it exactly replicated in other religious traditions. However, some of the symbols of baptism, such as naming, water and light are common to religions. Also, many religions have birth customs to which you can introduce the children. If you bear these points in mind, there are many possible ways of extending this work.

Naming

Look at how parents choose names in other religious traditions. In Islam there tend to be two types of first names. One of these is the religious name. Muslim parents often take names from the family of the prophet Mohammed or the ninety-nine names of Allah. The local imam (religious leader) is often asked to choose the name. There may be, also, a personal name which can be the same as the religious name. Many personal names are those of past prophets or important religious leaders such as Ibrahim or Fatima. Usually Muslims choose names to remind them of their faith.

● Sikh babies are named when they are taken to the gurdwara for the first time. The holy book, the Guru Granth Sahib, is read and when the reader opens the book the child is given a name which begins with the first letter on the page. This ceremony is called Nam Rakha. Many Sikh personal names have a religious significance, for example Gurbachan (the word of the Guru) or Amrit (holy water). Sikh surnames often relate to geographical areas or villages in India. The special names of Singh for males, meaning lion, and Kaur for females, meaning princess, were introduced by the tenth Guru, Gobind Singh, in

1699. You may like to tell the children this story which is now remembered at the Sikh festival of Baisakhi. (You can find this story in most books about Sikhism, for example, *The Living Religions Series*, published by Thomas Nelson) The children may also like to act it out.

● Hindus give names to their children in a special ceremony called Nam Sankar. This takes place at the mandir (temple) or at home about six weeks after the birth. There are readings from the Geeta or the Vedas (holy scriptures). Ghee (clarified butter) and herbs are burnt over a flame to purify the air. The child is blessed and the name is announced to all present. Books on world religions will give you extra information.

● A Jewish boy is given his Hebrew names when he is circumcised, eight days after birth. This is to remember the covenant (or agreement) made between God and Abraham, on behalf of the Jewish people, and recorded in Genesis, chapter 17, verses 10–11. The Hebrew term for this ceremony is Brit Milah. Many families will not announce the baby's name until after the brit has been performed.

Learn about birth customs

There are other birth customs in religious traditions which are well worth exploring. For reference see, for example, *Birth Customs* by Jon Mayled or *Birth Customs* by Lucy Rushton (Wayland). Photopacks such as the Westhill faith packs contain good large photographs and helpful text about this subject. Refer to the list of 'Resources and suppliers' opposite.

Explore water as a symbol in religions

It is possible to look at the use of water as symbolically cleansing. Be careful when concentrating on this to keep a clear focus. In Islam, the practice of Wudu before prayer can be explored. In Sikhism, people bathe before worship. In India, Sikh gurdwaras have a large pool for this. The practice goes back to Guru Nanak who used to go to the river to bathe before prayer. Be careful not to extend this too far or the concept of making clean may become obscured by general references to water.

Explore light as a symbol

This provides many opportunities. You could look at worship, for example, candles in Christian Churches, the aarti lamp and divas in Hinduism, the Ner Tamid (eternal light) found in many synagogues to remind Jews of God's eternal presence. Of course there are also the festivals of light but, again, it may be preferable to keep it simple and focus on light as a symbol.

Resources and suppliers

Articles of Faith, 0161 763 6232
BFSS National RE Centre, Brunel University at the Osterley Campus, 0181 891 8324
National Society's RE Centre, 0171 932 1190
PCET (Pictorial Charts Educational Trust), 0181 567 5343
Westhill RE Centre, Birmingham, 0121 415 2258
Welsh National RE Centre, 01248 382952
ICOREC, 0161 248 5731

Assessment

When you have finished this topic you will have a fairly good idea whether the children have enjoyed it. You should also be able to judge by the outcomes how much they have learned. Evaluation can take the following form:

What do they know?

There is an enormous amount of information that the children may have learned. From this topic, the majority of Year 2 children might be expected to know:

- what baptism is for;
- the names of relevant baptism artefacts;
- what a church is for and what happens in one.

What can they do?

In a typical mixed ability group it will be expected that children will respond at different levels to the same question or issue. For this topic all or most pupils can be expected to be familiar with the way in which the Christian community nurtures its young children. You can expect the majority of children to be able to describe the baptism ceremony. You might also expect some children to describe how baptism marks the start of someone's life as a member of the church.

All or most children should be able to:

- recognise buildings as churches;
- recognise some examples of church furniture;
- recognise a Christian act of worship.

What have they experienced?

The children should have:

- handled religious artefacts sensitively;
- visited a church and behaved in an appropriate manner;
- talked to people connected with the church and/or the baptism of infants.

How have they made their knowledge public?

The children should have made a public display of their knowledge through writing, art, drama. They should also have behaved and asked questions in an appropriate way to visitors and on visits.

Religious education